MAX notes®

Geoffrey Chaucer's

The Canterbury Tales

Text by
Sarah Ray Voelker
(B.S. Ed., University of Arkansas)
Chair, Language Arts Department
Green B. Trimble Technical High School
Fort Worth, Texas

Research & Education Association

Dr. M. Fogiel, Director

MAXnotes® for
THE CANTERBURY TALES

Printed in the United States of America

Library of Congress Control Number 2003103994

International Standard Book Number 0-87891-994-5

MAXnotes® is a registered trademark of
Research & Education Association, Piscataway, New Jersey 08854

What **MAXnotes®** *Will Do for You*

This book is intended to help you absorb the essential contents and features of Geoffrey Chaucer's *Canterbury Tales* and to help you gain a thorough understanding of the work. The book has been designed to do this more quickly and effectively than any other study guide.

For best results, this **MAXnotes** book should be used as a companion to the actual work, not instead of it. The interaction between the two will greatly benefit you.

To help you in your studies, this book presents the most up-to-date interpretations of every section of the actual work, followed by questions and fully explained answers that will enable you to analyze the material critically. The questions also will help you to test your understanding of the work and will prepare you for discussions and exams.

Meaningful illustrations are included to further enhance your understanding and enjoyment of the literary work. The illustrations are designed to place you into the mood and spirit of the work's settings.

The **MAXnotes** also include summaries, character lists, explanations of plot, and section-by-section analyses. A biography of the author and discussion of the work's historical context will help you put this literary piece into the proper framework of what is taking place.

The use of this study guide will save you the hours of preparation time that would ordinarily be required to arrive at a complete grasp of this work of literature. You will be well prepared for classroom discussions, homework, and exams. The guidelines that are included for writing papers and reports on various topics will prepare you for any added work which may be assigned.

The **MAXnotes** will take your grades "to the max."

Dr. Max Fogiel
Program Director

Contents

**Each book includes List of Characters,
Summary, Analysis, Study Questions and
Answers, and Suggested Essay Topics.**

MAXnotes are simply the best - but don't just take our word for it

"... I have told every bookstore in the area to carry your MAXnotes. They are the only notes I recommend to my students. There is no comparison between MAXnotes and all other notes ..."
  – *High School Teacher & Reading Specialist,*
  Arlington High School, Arlington, MA

"... I discovered the MAXnotes when a friend loaned me her copy of the MAXnotes for Romeo and Juliet... The book really helped me understand the story. Please send me a list of stores in my area that carry the MAXnotes. I would like to use more of them ..."
  – *Student, San Marino, CA*

"... The two MAXnotes titles that I have used have been very, very, helpful in helping me understand the subject matter reviewed. Thank you for creating the MAXnotes series ..."
  – *Student, Morrisville, PA*

A Glance at Some of the Characters

The Priest

The Cook

The Monk

The Wife of Bath

The Friar

The Cleric

The Franklin

The Physician

Introduction

The Life and Work of Geoffrey Chaucer

Living in the "Age of Information," it is sometimes a surprise to modern readers to learn how little is actually known of Geoffrey Chaucer, now called the Father of English literature. The precise year of his birth is not even known; it is generally listed as "between 1340 and 1345." However, since knowledge of an author's life is helpful in understanding his work, what little of Chaucer's life is recorded is summarized here.

Chaucer's father, John, was a wealthy wine merchant who provided handsomely for his family. They lived in the Vintry District of London, a prosperous and fashionable area. John Chaucer sent his son to St. Paul's Almonery School where Geoffrey received a fine classical education with instruction in Latin, rhetoric, religion, philosophy, science, and French, the language of the court.

When Chaucer was in his very early teens, his father obtained a position at court for him where he was to serve in the household of Elizabeth, Countess of Ulster, who was the wife of King Edward III's second son, the Duke of Clarence. Such a position was highly desirable for a medieval youth, as it would aid him in his future. It was an opportunity for him to experience life in a noble household, to travel, to learn courtly manners, and to become acquainted with politics and government.

Also in the service of Elizabeth was Philippa Payne de Roet, daughter of the Flemish knight Sir Payne de Roet who served John of Gaunt. Chaucer married the young lady-in-waiting in 1366, an important alliance for him. His new wife was a member of the minor nobility and the duke that her father served could, and did, become an influential patron for Geoffrey Chaucer.

Apparently, the gifted young Chaucer did well as a page, for by 1359 he had been advanced to military service with the Duke of Clarence. In the Duke's service, Chaucer went on a campaign to France and was captured by the French. He had to be ransomed by the King.

No more specifics are known of Chaucer's life until he is named in the household records of King Edward III in 1367. At that time, Edward granted him an annuity for life (an annual income) referring to Chaucer as "our beloved valet."

It is not known what Chaucer had done to endear himself to the ruler, but Chaucer seems to have been extremely valuable to the royal family by whom he was retained all of his life. Not only did he fight for the Duke of Clarence, he also served in battle in France with John of Gaunt, King Edward's third son, in 1369. John granted Chaucer an additional lifetime annuity in 1374. By that time, Chaucer had published his first work, *The Book of the Duchess*, a beautiful elegy consoling John on the death of his first wife, Blanche. The connection with John of Gaunt was likely enhanced when Philippa Chaucer's sister, Katherine Roet Swyford, became John of Gaunt's mistress and eventually his third wife.

Geoffrey Chaucer was obviously skilled politically, but his diplomatic abilities were also useful to the royal family. In 1372, he was sent on his first diplomatic mission to Italy. It was probably while in Italy that Chaucer became acquainted with the works of the Italian poets Boccaccio, Petrarch, and Dante, all of whom extensively influenced his own writing.

Returning to England in 1374, Chaucer was named Controller of Customs for the Port of London, which gave him entire administrative authority for England's most important industry, the wool trade. He served in this capacity until 1386. During this time, he was sent to Italy and France on several diplomatic missions for the King.

It is quite remarkable that between 1370 and 1386, in addition to his demanding career in the King's service, Chaucer also wrote and published four major works of literature: *The Book of the*

Duchess, already mentioned; *The Parliament of Fowls*, an elaborate discourse on the nature of love; *The House of Fame*, an ironic commentary on nearly all of medieval pedagogy with the retelling of a famous classical romance; and *Troilus and Criseyde*, a long serious love poem. He had completed an English translation of a well-known French poem, *Le Roman de la Rose*, and a prose translation of Boethius' *The Consolations of Philosophy*. Chaucer also wrote and published in *The Legend of Good Women: A Life of St. Cecelia*, which later became one of the Canterbury Tales.

In 1385 Chaucer was transferred to Kent, where he served as Justice of the Peace and was elected to Parliament. He returned to London in 1389 when he was appointed Clerk of the King's Works for Westminster and the Tower of London. In this position, Chaucer had complete supervision of the construction of these two monumental structures. He was, in fact, buried in Westminster cathedral, the first to be so honored by burial in what has become known as "The Poet's Corner."

The Canterbury Tales, Geoffrey Chaucer's masterpiece, was undertaken in 1387, but was never completed. Work on it ended with Chaucer's death on October 25, 1400.

Historical Background

The Canterbury Tales is set in fourteenth-century London, one of the medieval period's great centers of commerce and culture. In England at this time, society was still very strictly ordered, with the King and nobles having all power in things political and the Catholic Church having all authority in spiritual matters. However, trade and commerce with other nations had expanded dramatically in this century, giving rise to a new and highly vocal middle class composed of merchants, traders, shopkeepers, and skilled craftsmen. Their newly acquired wealth, their concentration in centers of commerce, and their organization into guilds gave this newly emerging class increasing power and influence.

However, the population of England remained for the most part agrarian, poor peasants working hard for a meager living farming on rented land, completely at the mercy of the landowner, mired in ignorance and superstition, and generally devoid of any opportunity to change their lot in life. These peasant people looked to the Church for consolation and defense. Sometimes they found nurture there, though, just as often, they confronted corruption and further victimization. As the clergy became landowners, they victimized the peasants as blatantly as did the nobility. The hierarchical organization of the Church and its dominance of education also gave rise to widespread shocking abuse and corruption.

In the latter fourteenth century, there was a new and considerable resistance to the inflexible dominance of society by the nobility and the clergy. The Plague had struck three times in the century, killing one-third of the population of England. The resultant labor shortage at last gave the peasants the courage to insist on higher wages. They even staged what is known as "The Peasants' Rebellion" in 1381 in reaction to their enforced poverty, but their group was quickly subdued by the nobility.

Geoffrey Chaucer witnessed this rebellion firsthand. He was the Controller of the Custom in London and resided rent-free in a house built onto the wall around London. His house was located just over the gate where the furious peasants descended on the city. One can only imagine his horror as he watched the rebels burn the elaborate castle of his patron, John of Gaunt.

Chaucer's ability to give the reader his view of life in the city of London is but one of the sterling elements of *The Canterbury Tales*. Chaucer knew these angry peasants and successful and outspoken merchants and tradesmen because he lived among them and dealt with them constantly in his work. His service to the nobility and his diplomatic duties gave him wide acquaintance among the clergy and the ruling class. All of these types of people are recreated in *The Canterbury Tales*, giving the reader an almost perfect picture of life in medieval England.

Aside from the living people of England, the other major influences on *The Canterbury Tales* were the vast and widely varied works of literature with which Chaucer was unusually well-acquainted. Since he alludes so often to his sources in *The Canterbury Tales*, it is certain that Chaucer was familiar with all the classical writers, such as Ovid and Virgil, and with the Christian apologists like Augustine and Boethius. He knew and corresponded with the French poet Descartes, and had studied French literature extensively. Unlike most of his English contemporaries, Chaucer was a devotee of the Italian poets Dante and Petrarch. He seems to have been greatly influenced by the Italian poet Boccaccio, as well; *The Canterbury Tales* has many elements in common with Boccaccio's *Decameron*.

That Chaucer used many well-known models and sources for his tales, Chaucer himself admits. However, with *The Canterbury Tales*, Chaucer departed from the prevailing literary norm which held that all worthy writing was modelled on a work already in existence. While all of his tales contain elements borrowed from classical models, Chaucer's stories are all dramatically altered in some way so that they become something new, rather than a repetition of an old pattern. Few of his pilgrims are copies; they are essentially English; and the framing of the tales with a trip to Canterbury is a Chaucerian innovation which sets him apart totally from his predecessors.

One of the things that makes *The Canterbury Tales* unique is the frame just mentioned. As the title implies, *The Canterbury Tales* is a collection of all sorts of stories, but they are ingeniously united by being framed by a journey and told by the travellers on the journey. A frame of sorts existed in Boccaccio's *Decameron*, but Chaucer's use of this device is original in its completeness, polish, and brilliance.

The work is also remarkable because it is written in English. In Chaucer's day, it was a foregone conclusion that all serious writing had to be done in Latin or French. Chaucer himself was fluent in both these languages, as well as in Italian. Yet his long experimentation with poetry written in these languages convinced him that it was not only possible, but desirable, to make poetic music in the vernacular, which, for him, was Middle English.

This work was well-received. This is known because enough handwritten copies of it were in circulation for the famous printer William Caxton to make *The Canterbury Tales* one of the first works he printed when he imported his first printing press in 1478. Enough demand for the book existed for him to print a second edition in 1483; it must have been extremely popular, for both printing and purchasing books were very expensive at that time. Only a widely read and widely accepted book would have been given a second printing. *The Canterbury Tales* has never been out of print since that time.

Master List of Characters

The Narrator—*Geoffrey Chaucer, the author, although he is never named*

The Knight—*father of the Squire; lord of the Yeoman (minor nobility)*

The Squire—*young man of 20, son of the Knight (minor nobility)*

The Yeoman—*a forester; servant of the Knight (peasant class)*

The Prioress—*superior of a monastery of nuns; attended by the Nun, the Monk, the Friar, and the Priest (clergy)*

The Monk—*manages the estates of the Prioress and the monastery (clergy)*

The Friar—*a religious who has taken a vow of poverty and is licensed to beg (clergy)*

The Nun—*chaplain to the Prioress (clergy)*

The Priest—*with the Prioress; not described (clergy)*

The Merchant—*wealthy and pompous (middle class)*

The Cleric—*a religious who is a scholar at Oxford (clergy)*

The Man of Law—*a lawyer, shrewd and wealthy (middle class)*

The Franklin—*landowner; wealthy (middle class; possibly minor nobility)*

The Haberdasher—*hat and clothing maker; guildsman (middle class)*

The Carpenter—*guildsman (middle class)*

The Weaver—*makes fabric; guildsman (middle class)*

The Dyer—*dyes fabric and leather; guildsman (middle class)*

The Tapestry-Maker—*makes large, intricate woven pictures which are decorative and expensive; guildsman (middle class)*

The Cook—*works for the five guildsmen (peasant class)*

The Shipman—*a sailor, commander of a merchant ship (middle class)*

The Physician—*well-educated; a lover of gold (middle class)*

The Wife of Bath—*has survived five husbands; prosperous, gregarious, experienced (middle class)*

The Parson—*poor because he is good; a true pastor (clergy)*

The Plowman—*brother of the Parish Priest; an honest, decent farmer (peasant)*

The Miller—*owns a mill; grinds grain into meal and flour (middle class)*

The Manciple—*a buyer for 30 lawyers who are administrators of London courts (middle class)*

The Reeve—*manager of a nobleman's estate; prosperous (middle class)*

The Summoner—*an agent of the Church courts who summons sinners to answer charges before the court (clergy)*

The Pardoner—*traded on the gullibility of the populace; sold relics and indulgences (which are pardons from the punishment due to sin) (clergy)*

The Host—*owner of the Tabard Inn where all the pilgrims meet; self-appointed leader; tour guide for the pilgrims (middle class)*

*The Canon—*a clergyman, generally in charge of a cathedral (clergy)*

*The Canon's Yeoman—*servant to the Canon (peasant)*

> **The last two characters join the group when the journey is almost over.*

Summary of the Poem

In the beauty of April, the Narrator and 29 oddly assorted travelers happen to meet at the Tabard Inn in Southwark, London. This becomes the launching point for their 60-mile, four-day religious journey to the shrine of St. Thomas à Becket at the Cathedral in Canterbury. Great blessing and forgiveness were to be heaped upon those who made the pilgrimage; relics of the saint were enshrined there, and miracles had been reported by those who prayed before the shrine. Chaucer's pilgrims, however, are not all traveling for religious reasons. Many of them simply enjoy social contact or the adventure of travel.

As the travelers are becoming acquainted, their Host, the inn-keeper Harry Bailley, decides to join them. He suggests that they pass the time along the way by telling stories. Each pilgrim is to tell four stories—two on the way to Canterbury, and two on the return trip—a total of 120 stories. He will furnish dinner at the end of the trip to the one who tells the best tale. The framework is thus laid out for the organization of *The Canterbury Tales*.

Chaucer, the Narrator, observes all of the characters as they are arriving and getting acquainted. He describes in detail most of the travelers who represent a cross-section of fourteenth-century English society. All levels are represented, beginning with the Knight who is the highest-ranking character socially. Several levels of holiness and authority in the clergy are among the pilgrims while the majority of the characters are drawn from the middle class. A small number of the peasant class are also making the journey, most of them as servants to other pilgrims.

As the travelers begin their journey the next morning, they draw straws to see who will tell the first tale. The Knight draws the shortest straw. He begins the storytelling with a long romantic epic about two brave young knights who both fall in love with the same woman and who spend years attempting to win her love.

Everyone enjoys the tale and they agree that the trip is off to an excellent start. When the Host invites the Monk to tell a story to match the Knight's, the Miller, who is drunk, becomes so rude and insistent that he be allowed to go next that the Host allows it. The Miller's tale is indeed very funny, involving several tricks and a very dirty prank as a young wife conspires with her lover to make love to him right under her husband's nose.

The Miller's fabliau upsets the Reeve because it involves an aging carpenter being cuckolded by his young wife, and the Reeve himself is aging and was formerly a carpenter. Insulted by the Miller, the Reeve retaliates with a tale about a miller who is made a fool of in very much the same manner as the carpenter in the preceding rendition.

After the Reeve, the Cook speaks up and begins to tell another humorous adventure about a thieving, womanizing young apprentice. Chaucer did not finish writing this story; it stops almost at the beginning.

When the dialogue among the travelers resumes, the morning is half gone and the Host, Harry Bailley, urges the Man of Law to begin his entry quickly. Being a lawyer, the Man of Law is very long-winded and relates a very long story about the life of a noblewoman named Constance who suffers patiently and virtuously through a great many terrible trials. In the end she is rewarded for her perseverance.

The Man of Law's recital, though lengthy, has pleased the other pilgrims very much. Harry Bailley then calls upon the Parson to tell a similar tale of goodness; but the Shipman, who wants to hear no more sermonizing, says he will take his turn next and will tell a merry story without a hint of preaching. Indeed, his story involves a lovely wife who cuckolds her husband to get money for a new dress and gets away with the whole affair.

Evidently looking for contrast in subject matter, the Host next invites the Prioress to give them a story. Graciously, she relates a short legend about a little schoolboy who is martyred and through whose death a miracle takes place.

After hearing this miraculous narrative, all of the travelers become very subdued, so the Host calls upon the Narrator (Chaucer) to liven things up. Slyly making fun of the Host's literary pretensions, Chaucer recites a brilliant parody on knighthood composed in low rhyme. Harry hates Chaucer's poem and interrupts to complain; again in jest, Chaucer tells a long, boring version of an ancient myth. However, the Host is very impressed by the serious moral tone of this inferior tale and is highly complimentary.

Since the myth just told involved a wise and patient wife, Harry Bailley takes this opportunity to criticize his own shrewish wife. He then digresses further with a brief commentary on monks which leads him to call upon the pilgrim Monk for his contribution to the entertainment.

The Monk belies his fun-loving appearance by giving a disappointing recital about famous figures who are brought low by fate. The Monk's subject is so dreary that the Knight stops him, and the Host berates him for lowering the morale of the party. When the Monk refuses to change his tone, the Nun's Priest accepts the Host's request for a happier tale. The Priest renders the wonderful fable of Chanticleer, a proud rooster taken in by the flattery of a clever fox.

Harry Bailley is wildly enthusiastic about the Priest's tale, turning very bawdy in his praise. The earthy Wife of Bath is chosen as the next participant, probably because the Host suspects that she will continue in the same bawdy vein. However, the Wife turns out to be quite a philosopher, prefacing her tale with a long discourse on marriage. When she does tell her tale, it is about the marriage of a young and virile knight to an ancient hag.

When the Wife has concluded, the Friar announces that he will tell a worthy tale about a summoner. He adds that everyone knows there is nothing good to say about summoners and tells a story which proves his point.

Infuriated by the Friar's insulting tale, the Summoner first tells a terrible joke about friars and then a story which condemns them, too. His rendering is quite coarse and dirty.

Hoping for something more uplifting next, the Host gives the Cleric his chance, reminding the young scholar not to be too scholarly and to put in some adventure. Obligingly, the Cleric entertains with his tale of the cruel Walter of Saluzzo who tested his poor wife unmercifully.

The Cleric's tale reminds the Merchant of his own unhappy marriage and his story reflects his state. It is yet another tale of a bold, unfaithful wife in a marriage with a much older man.

When the Merchant has finished, Harry Bailley again interjects complaints about his own domineering wife, but then requests a love story of the Squire. The young man begins an exotic tale that promises to be a fine romance, but Chaucer did not complete this story, so it is left unfinished.

The dialogue resumes with the Franklin complimenting the Squire and trying to imitate his eloquence with an ancient lyric of romance.

There is no conversation among the pilgrims before the Physician's tale. His story is set in ancient Rome and concerns a young virgin who prefers death to dishonor.

The Host has really taken the Physician's sad story to heart and begs the Pardoner to lift his spirits with a happier tale. However, the other pilgrims want something more instructive, so the

Pardoner obliges. After revealing himself to be a very wicked man, the Pardoner instructs the company with an allegory about vice leading three young men to their deaths. When he is finished, the Pardoner tries to sell his fake relics to his fellow travelers, but the Host prevents him, insulting and angering him in the process. The Knight has to intervene to restore peace.

The Second Nun then tells the moral and inspiring life story of St. Cecelia. About five miles later, a Canon and his Yeoman join the party, having ridden madly to catch up. Conversation reveals these men to be outlaws of sorts, but they are made welcome and invited to participate in the storytelling all the same. When the Canon's Yeoman reveals their underhanded business, the Canon rides off in a fit of anger, and the Canon's Yeoman relates a tale about a cheating alchemist, really a disclosure about the Canon.

It is late afternoon by the time the Yeoman finishes and the Cook has become so drunk that he falls off his horse. There is an angry interchange between the Cook and the Manciple, and the Cook has to be placated with more wine. The Manciple then tells his story, which is based on an ancient myth and explains why the crow is black.

At sundown the Manciple ends his story. The Host suggests that the Parson conclude the day of tale-telling with a fable. However, the Parson preaches a two-hour sermon on penitence instead. *The Canterbury Tales* ends here.

Although Chaucer actually completed only about one-fifth of the proposed 120 tales before his death, *The Canterbury Tales* reflects all the major types of medieval literature. They are defined for the reader as follows:

Romance: a narrative in metrical verse; tales of love, adventure, knightly combat, and ceremony

Fabliaux: stories based on trickery and deception; often involve adultery

Myth: a story originating in classical literature

Breton Lais: a type of fairy tale; set in the Brittany province of France; contains fairies, elves, folk wisdom, and folktales

Beast Fable: animals personify human qualities and act out human situations; usually teaches a lesson

Sermon: a Christian lesson

Exemplum: a story which teaches a well-known lesson

Saint's Legend: inspiring story of the life and death of a saint

Miracle Story: one in which a saint or the Virgin Mary intervenes with a miracle in response to the faithfulness of a follower

Allegory: a tale in which persons represent abstract qualities; i.e., Death, Virtue, Love

Mock Romance: parodies, or makes fun of, the usual subjects of a romance

These genres are further explained in the analyses of individual tales.

Estimated Reading Time

The length of time necessary to read the entire work will depend on whether it is being read in Modern or Middle English. The reading in Modern English will go much faster; probably an hour for the prologue and an hour for The Knight's Tale, with the remainder of the tales requiring 30 to 45 minutes each.

If the student is required to read the work in Middle English, with all the footnotes for interpretation, each part named above will take about twice as long. The reader can estimate a total of 14 hours for the Modern English version, or 28 hours for the Middle English.

It is strongly suggested that the book be divided by the reader into manageable units for sittings of no more than two hours.

The Canterbury Tales

General Prologue

New Characters:

The Narrator: *Geoffrey Chaucer, the author, although he is never named*

The Knight: *father of the Squire; lord of the Yeoman*

The Squire: *young man of 20, son of the Knight*

The Yeoman: *a forester; servant of the Knight*

The Prioress: *superior of a monastery of nuns; attended by the Nun, the Monk, the Friar, and the Priest*

The Monk: *manages the estates of the Prioress and the monastery*

The Friar: *a religious who has taken a vow of poverty and is licensed to beg*

The Nun: *chaplain to the Prioress*

The Priest: *with the Prioress; not described*

The Merchant: *wealthy and pompous*

The Cleric: *a religious who is a scholar at Oxford*

The Man of Law: *shrewd and wealthy*

The Franklin: *landowner; wealthy*

The Haberdasher: *hat and clothing maker; guildsman*

The Carpenter: *guildsman*

The Weaver: *makes fabric; guildsman*

The Dyer: *dyes fabric and leather; guildsman*

The Tapestry-Maker: *makes large, intricate woven pictures which are decorative and expensive; guildsman*

The Cook: *works for the five guildsmen*

The Shipman: *commander of a merchant ship*

The Physician: *well-educated; a lover of gold*

The Wife of Bath: *has survived five husbands; prosperous, gregarious, experienced*

The Parson: *poor because he is good; a true pastor*

The Plowman: *brother of the Parish Priest; an honest, decent farmer*

The Miller: *owns a mill; grinds grain into meal and flour*

The Manciple: *a buyer for 30 lawyers who are administrators of London courts*

The Reeve: *manager of a nobleman's estate; prosperous*

The Summoner: *an agent of the Church courts who summons sinners to answer charges before the court*

The Pardoner: *traded on the gullibility of the populace; sold relics and indulgences (which are pardons from the punishment due to sin)*

The Host: *owner of the Tabard Inn where all the pilgrims meet; self-appointed leader; tour guide for the pilgrims*

Summary

Chaucer begins the Prologue with a beautiful announcement of spring. This introduction is the voice of the Poet, polished, elegant, and finished. He tells us that just as Nature has a predictable course through the seasons, so does human nature follow a seasonal pattern which causes people to want to break out of winter's confinement and go traveling in the spring.

Thus the stage is set for Chaucer, who is the Narrator of this poem. Twenty-nine travelers meet at the Tabard Inn in London before undertaking a journey to the Shrine of St. Thomas à Becket

in Canterbury. The group is assembling as Chaucer arrives and, as he observes the group and interacts with some of them, he decides that he will join their party. From his vantage point as anonymous Narrator, Chaucer describes the scene and the pilgrims as they arrive.

The Knight is introduced first, which is appropriate as he is the highest ranking character socially. This old soldier has spent a lifetime fighting battles for Christianity all over the world and has consistently distinguished himself. He is dedicated to the knightly ideal of chivalry, courtesy, truth, honor, and generosity.

Accompanying the Knight is his 20-year-old son, the Squire, who is very much in contrast to his father. While he has been in a few skirmishes, "to impress his lady," the Squire is obviously still young and inexperienced. He is dressed in the height of fashion with carefully arranged curls. Devoted to the rituals of courting, the Squire appears to be in love with love.

The Yeoman is a servant to the Knight. He is a forester, in charge of the Knight's woodlands and appears to be the ideal simple, loyal peasant; yet he is so well-equipped with elaborate weapons and perfect arrows that his simplicity is suspect. When the Narrator adds that the forester understood all the tricks of woodcraft, he seems to be suggesting that the Yeoman is profiting in some way as he manages forests which are not his.

The next group of pilgrims arrives with the Prioress, Madame Eglantine. While obviously intelligent and able, the Prioress is described as being very concerned that others view her as ladylike and refined. She is apparently tenderhearted to the point of sentimentality.

The Prioress is accompanied by the Nun, who is her chaplain. The reader is told nothing about the Nun or about the Priest who is also with the Prioress. Her estate manager, the Monk, however, is vividly described. He is very careless of his religious vows, devoting all of his time and energy to the management of the Prioress's estates. He manages them to prosper, though, so that he himself may be denied none of the pleasures and luxuries of the hunt.

The third priest in company with the Prioress is the Friar, wanton, merry, and quite irreligious. Supposedly sworn to helping the poor, Hubert grants absolution to anyone who gives him money, much of which he pockets rather than distributing it to the poor.

Socially, the middle class ranked third behind the nobility and the clergy; thus, the third type of character Chaucer presents is a successful and very busy Merchant who is representative of the rather recent prosperity and importance of his class. The Merchant talks of nothing but business and thinks himself an expert on all matters related to trade.

Following the Merchant, the Cleric arrives. He is very, very poorly dressed and mounted in stark contrast to other members of the clergy previously introduced. Unlike them, he is completely devoted to scholarship and oblivious to material wealth. He speaks primarily on moral themes.

The Man of Law is another sterling representative of the middle class who comes next under the Narrator's scrutiny. All of the Man of Law's great skill in legal matters is detailed; his wealth is reported; yet the Narrator confides that although the man brags constantly about how busy he is with his cases, his "busy-ness" may be more imagined than real.

With the Man of Law is the Franklin, who is a wealthy land-owner who lives for his own sensual pleasure. The delights of the table obsess this gentleman. As an aside, the reader is told that he has served as a justice of the peace and a member of Parliament, but these are only incidental as far as he is concerned.

Grouped together next are five wealthy and important crafts-men, all officials in their guilds. These include the Haberdasher, the Carpenter, the Weaver, the Dyer, and the Tapestry-Maker. It is implied that all of these men curry favor with their wives who would have been highly unpleasant had not their husbands prospered.

The guildsmen have brought their own Cook. Apparently, he is quite able and experienced, but repugnant to the Narrator because he has a large sore on his leg. To medieval observers such an affliction rendered a person unclean and undesirable.

The Sailor, or Shipman, is described next. He rides his horse so poorly that it is obvious the man is much more comfortable on the sea than on the land. On board ship, however, the Shipman is expert, knowledgeable, and successful. He has surmounted many storms on the sea, but at the same time he has taken advantage of the merchants who use his vessel to ship their goods. In fact, he is reported to have no scruples at all.

There is a Physician among the pilgrims. Chaucer tells the reader of his great learning, yet holds him in contempt because this doctor loves gold so much and overcharges his patients for remedies that do them no good. For all his great learning, this Physician has not studied the Bible, the implication being that he lacks the concern and mercy of the true healer.

The Wife of Bath, the third of the female pilgrims, is introduced next. She is quite outrageous and is one of the most famous characters in all of literature. Slightly deaf and with gaps between her teeth, the Wife wears an incredible and ostentatious outfit. The Wife is skilled at weaving and is extremely prosperous. She has survived five husbands and is said to have great knowledge about love. Reportedly good-humored and full of life, the Wife of Bath is going to Canterbury to find her sixth husband.

Behind the raucous Wife of Bath comes the Parson, a poor and humble priest who is devoted to his parishioners and serves them faithfully and well. He teaches the Gospel by his example and is never severe with sinners. With the Parson is his brother, the Plowman, a decent and hardworking peasant, similar in nature and goodness to the Parson.

The burly, red-haired Miller is juxtaposed beside the two preceding, mild-mannered travelers. He is large and exceptionally strong, with a bulbous nose and a generally ugly appearance. His manners and conversation are as coarse as his appearance; in addition, the Miller is none too honest with his customers.

The Manciple (Maunciple) is a friendly fellow whose job is to do the purchasing and keep the accounts for a group of 30 lawyers. This friendly fellow has tricked his employers by embezzling profits in his shady deals for them, leaving them to live frugally as he spends the money he stole from them.

Next comes the Reeve, a comical-looking man who is very skinny with legs like long sticks. Like the Manciple, the Reeve manages the affairs of another man, a wealthy landowner in this case. The Reeve has grown so rich in this post that the owner of the estate has to come to his employee to borrow money.

The Summoner is another corrupt member of the clergy who is presented after the Reeve. He is an official of the Church court who calls sinners to answer charges before it. For enough money, he will see that sins are not reported. The Summoner has an ugly, pimply face and is a drunk and a lecher.

The Pardoner is as unscrupulous as the Summoner. He is fresh from Rome with a bagful of indulgences (which are pardons from the punishment due to sin) which he will sell rather than grant to those who have done penance. He also has many outrageous fake relics which he will gladly sell. The Pardoner even sings loudly and well in church to get people to put more money in the offering, most of which he will retain.

After all these travelers have been described, the Narrator apologizes if any of his descriptions are so crude that they offend the reader, but excuses himself by commenting that Christ Himself was very plainspoken. Although the Narrator has joined the group, he tells us nothing of himself.

The final description in the Prologue is of Harry Bailley, the Host (innkeeper) who is very genial and sociable, fond of telling jokes. In the course of describing Bailley, the Narrator reports that the Host has offered to come along to Canterbury and to act as guide and leader of the party if they will all agree to be bound by his decisions. The pilgrims all agree, and further assent to his idea that each of them tell four stories along the way, two on the road to Canterbury and two on the return trip. Thus organized, the group retires for the night.

Analysis

The pilgrims assembling for Canterbury may be seen as a cross-section of medieval society, with all its richness and variety. Every stratum of society is represented. The Knight and his son are members of the nobility while the Plowman and the Yeoman are drawn from the peasant class. The majority of the travelers, however, represent the vigorous new middle class of England. Such characters as the Man of Law, the Merchant, the Wife of Bath, and the Shipman personify this group: energetic and prosperous, materialistic, and somewhat self-conscious as they display the trappings of their newly acquired wealth and status.

The clergy is also very much in evidence with the enormous wealth and power of the Catholic Church reflected in their holdings and their extensive authority. The Prioress, for example, is mistress of so large and rich an estate that she is able to travel with four retainers. The Pardoner and the Summoner have the authority to forgive sin and remit punishment, but at the same time, as they sell what they are supposed to give, both of these clergymen symbolize the widespread corruption rampant in the medieval Church.

The characters are far more than mere representative types, however. Chaucer describes each of them so graphically that each traveler becomes not only a stereotype, but also an individual. The Merchant, for example, has acquired wealth and prestige and pride typical of the successful middle class businessman, but he is also described as a risk-taker. He plays the market, so to speak; and he never talks about his financial affairs. This small bit of extra information—the telling comment—supplied by Chaucer for nearly every character—adds the extra dimension to the character, which individualizes him/her.

With the Cleric, it is the knowledge that "...gladly would he learn and gladly teach"; with the Wife of Bath, it is the information that she is gap-toothed and that she will allow no other woman to go ahead of her at the offertory which is most revealing. Setting each character apart in this manner is universally considered one of the most brilliant of Chaucer's devices.

Later, the reader will observe that Chaucer amplifies each character further through the story that the character tells. The overly sensitive Prioress, for instance, will tell a highly sentimental miracle story while the crude, dishonest Miller will tell a dirty tale involving trickery. In other words, Chaucer uses the story the character selects as a further means of describing and individualizing each pilgrim. The reader should be alert to this device as it is one of *The Canterbury Tales'* most outstanding features.

In addressing characterization, it should further be noted that Chaucer creates no character who is either totally good or completely evil. While good or evil may dominate, each pilgrim is also given some redeeming qualities. This duplicity certainly parallels real-life people and accounts to a large degree for the continued popularity of the work.

Chaucer, in the person of the Narrator, appears to want to assume an almost journalistic stance, merely reporting what he observes and seeming to refrain from judgment, leaving that function to the reader. While he appears unable to keep from poking fun at his characters, he also refrains from meanness and bitterness in describing them. The overall effect of this deliberate detachment is the jolly, playful mood appropriate to a group of Canterbury pilgrims setting off on their adventure.

Study Questions

1. How many pilgrims are making the journey to Canterbury?
2. Why are all these people going to Canterbury?
3. List the members of the middle class in the group.
4. List the members of the clergy.
5. Which members of the clergy appear to be corrupt or sinful?
6. What plan for the group does the Host propose?
7. How does Chaucer himself fit into the group?
8. By what devices does Chaucer reveal his characters?
9. How many of the tales did Chaucer actually complete?
10. What weaknesses within the Church do the pilgrim clergy represent?

Answers

1. There are 30 characters including Chaucer and the Host.
2. They are going to the Shrine of St. Thomas à Becket at Canterbury. They hope to receive special blessings.
3. The middle class group consists of the following: the Merchant; the Man of Law; the Franklin; the Haberdasher; the Carpenter; the Weaver; the Dyer; the Tapestry-Maker; the Shipman; the Physician; the Wife of Bath; the Miller; the Manciple; the Reeve; and the Host.
4. The clergy members are as follow: the Prioress; the Monk; the Friar; the Nun; the Priest; the Cleric; the Parson; the Summoner; and the Pardoner.
5. The Monk, the Pardoner, the Friar, and the Summoner appear corrupt.

6. Each traveler will tell four stories: two on the way to Canterbury and two on the return trip.

7. Chaucer is the anonymous Narrator. He is also one of the pilgrims.

8. Chaucer reveals his characters by direct description, the telling comment, and the tale each traveler tells.

9. There are twenty-three tales, two of which are fragments.

10. The clergy represent corruption, greed, and abuse of power in the Church.

Suggested Essay Topics

1. Using Chaucer's Prologue to *The Canterbury Tales*, describe the rising middle class of fourteenth-century England. In the essay, include the variety of occupations, the degree of wealth, the level of education, and the beginnings of political power represented among the pilgrims.

2. Contrast a corrupt clergyman from the Prologue with the Parson.

3. Select three characters from the Prologue whom Chaucer seems to be satirizing (i.e., the Wife of Bath, the Summoner, the Prioress). Using some direct quotations, explain the satire.

The Knight's Tale

Summary

The travelers have drawn straws to see who will tell the first tale. The Knight draws the shortest straw and graciously launches the entertainment with his tale.

Part One: In ancient times there was a famous conquering duke named Theseus who was lord of Athens. As the story opens, Theseus has just conquered the Amazons and married their queen, Hipppolyta. Returning victorious to Athens, the Duke is accosted by a group of grieving widows begging for his help. These noble-women are all former residents of Thebes; their husbands have

been killed in battle with the victorious King Creon who has forbidden the women to bury their dead and who has piled the bodies of their husbands in a heap for the dogs to devour. Theseus is touched by their plea for help and filled with hatred for Creon. Theseus immediately abandons the victory parade and takes his army to Thebes to destroy the wicked Creon. He sends Hippolyta and her beautiful sister, Emily, back to Athens.

Theseus encounters Creon, kills him in knightly fashion, destroys the city of Thebes, and restores the bodies of their slain husbands to the widows. When his troops begin to pillage the bodies of the slain enemy, they find among the dead two badly wounded young knights, Arcite and Palamon. They are known to be of the royal house of Thebes and are taken to Theseus for judgment. Theseus sends the two youths to Athens to be imprisoned there for the rest of their lives with no possibility of ransom or release.

Some years pass with the two imprisoned in anguish and woe. Then one spring morning Palamon rises early and spies the gorgeous sister of Queen Hippolyta walking in the garden below. He falls instantly in love. As Palamon moans with passion, his cousin Arcite awakens and also glimpses Lady Emily walking in the garden. Arcite, too, is instantly smitten.

The two young men quarrel, Palamon claiming to have the greater right to love Emily since he saw her first; and Arcite countering with the ancient argument that his right was as great as Palamon's since all is fair in love and war. However, the argument stalemates when the two realize that their imprisonment prevents either of them from acting on their lust. When Perotheus, a friend of Theseus', comes to visit, he persuades Theseus to release Arcite from prison. The only condition of Arcite's freedom is that he must never return to any land ruled by Duke Theseus on pain of instant death. To this condition Arcite assents.

Part Two: Arcite travels back to Thebes, but he never knows a moment's peace. His intense love for Emily torments him. He neither eats nor sleeps for two years, and becomes thin and pale and weak—almost unrecognizable as he pines for his love.

One night Arcite dreams that Mercury, winged god, is with him, commanding him to be happy. Mercury tells Arcite to go to Athens where his grief will end. Arcite determines to do exactly as he has been ordered in the dream. Glancing into a mirror, he notes for the first time the enormous change in his appearance. It occurs to him that no one in Athens will recognize him now, he is so changed.

As Arcite expects, he is not recognized in Athens and is immediately able to obtain a minor position in Emily's household where he can see her every day. Here, he is known as Philostrate and becomes well-known for his hard work and courtesy. In fact, Philostrate (Arcite) becomes so beloved that Theseus promotes him to become a squire in the Duke's own chamber. Arcite spends four or five years in this manner.

During the seven years since Arcite's release, Palamon has suffered his love alone in prison. In May of the seventh year, Palamon, with the help of a friend, drugs a guard and breaks out of prison. Palamon plans to hide all day in a grove of trees and start for Thebes at nightfall. In Thebes, he hopes to raise an army to make war against Theseus. In this way, he would either win Emily's hand or be killed in the attempt.

By chance, Arcite rises early that same day and wanders into the same grove where Palamon is hiding. As Arcite sings and laments aloud for love of Emily, Palamon overhears him and reveals himself to Arcite. The two renew their feud. Arcite, the honorable knight, agrees to supply battle equipment for both of them. They will fight to the death the next day, resolving forever which of them will claim the beautiful Emily.

The next morning, both fully armed, Palamon and Arcite begin to fight madly. However, Destiny intervenes, sending Theseus, Emily, and Hippolyta to hunt the stag in the same grove where the rival lovers fight. When Theseus discovers the identities of the two warriors, he swears to execute them both.

However, Hippolyta is so touched by the enormous love the young men bear her sister that she prevails upon Theseus to soften his heart and understand the power of their love. Theseus relents and agrees to allow both men to be free for one year. During that time he will prepare an arena and arrange for a knightly tournament. Palamon and Arcite are to spend the intervening year recruiting 100 knights each to face each other in the tournament, the outcome of which will decide which man wins Emily's hand in marriage.

Part Three: Theseus builds a fabulous theater, a mile in circumference, for the tournament. He erects three temples on the grounds: one to Venus, the goddess of love; one to Mars, the god of war; and a third to Diana, goddess of the hunt and of maidens.

At the end of the year, both Arcite and Palamon return to Athens, each with 100 distinguished knights. Just before the battle, Arcite, Palamon, and Emily each worship at the shrine of his particular patron. Palamon prays at the temple of Venus and receives a sign that his wish will be granted. Before the shrine of Diana, Emily prays that she may be allowed to remain a virgin, but Diana appears and tells Emily that all the gods have decided that she must marry one of the lovelorn young men. Arcite worships at the shrine to Mars who gives him a sign that he will be victorious.

Inevitably, war breaks out among the gods once these conflicting promises are given. Jupiter intervenes and Saturn promises Venus that Palamon shall win Emily's hand.

Part Four: Before the tournament begins, Theseus decrees that no deadly weapon may be used in the tournament. The contest must be decided by force alone, for he will permit no deaths among so noble a company. Furthermore, if one leader is captured by the opposing force, the rival will immediately be declared the victor.

Toward sundown, Palamon is wounded and captured. Arcite is declared the winner. Venus is infuriated by this victory of Mars, so Pluto makes the earth erupt where Arcite sits in victory. Arcite is thrown from his horse and grievously injured. Within a few days, Arcite dies of his wounds, on his deathbed making peace with his cousin Palamon. A fabulous funeral is held to honor the slain lover; an extended period of mourning followed.

When the period of mourning was concluded, Theseus sends for Palamon and Emily. After a discourse in which he explains that the noble death of Arcite fulfilled the will of the great god Jupiter, Theseus prevails upon Emily to look with favor upon Palamon's years of devotion. The two are finally married and live in love and harmony all the rest of their days.

Analysis

In keeping with medieval custom, it is fitting that the Knight should tell the first tale as he is the highest ranking member of the company socially. He graciously accepts the shortest straw with chivalrous courtesy.

The Knight's Tale is an almost perfect example of a romance, containing nearly all the features characteristic of this form of narrative. First, the theme of the tale intertwines ideal love with chivalrous conduct. Both young men fall passionately in love with Emily, but their love is inspired by her perfect beauty and later by her virtue; their love has no hint of sensuality. Furthermore, all of the characters deal with one another in a manner completely chivalrous and honorable. The conflict between Arcite and Palamon arises only when Arcite betrays an oath to Palamon, continuing to declare his love for the same woman to whom Palamon has pledged eternal love. This choice was disloyal in a knight's code of conduct, but it is the only time any of the characters depart from the courtly ideal.

Secondly, the story is set in the romantic long ago, another characteristic of the romance. Although it is an obvious anachronism, these medieval knights act out their drama in ancient Greece where the mythic, pagan element enters the tale and takes control of the outcome. Venus, Mars, and Diana war with one another so that the characters become their pawns in a struggle among the gods. Destiny also plays an enormous part in this pagan setting. It is only by chance, or destiny, that the young cousins are found alive on the battlefield; it is by chance that they both glimpse Emily and fall in love with her at almost the same moment. Arcite and Palamon also meet in the grove of trees by chance. Destiny decrees that Theseus ride into that exact spot and prevent the two from murdering each other.

Finally, the wisdom and justice of the authority figure, Theseus; the long and dramatic struggle to win the hand of the beloved; and the settling of the quarrel through a test of combat are further features which distinguish The Knight's Tale as a romance.

Chaucer's enormous acquaintance with all of medieval literature is particularly evident in The Knight's Tale. It is based on Boccaccio's *Teseide*, however, Chaucer cut a great deal of the story and adapted its character to suit medieval times. At many points in the story, particularly in places where the characters speculate on questions relating to the nature of good and evil, the author has inserted speeches from Boethius' *The Consolations of Philosophy*. The use of Greek mythology has already been noted. These examples are good evidence of Geoffrey Chaucer's particular brilliance—his ability to meld disparate elements into stories with a quality of newness and uniqueness.

Study Questions

1. Why is it appropriate that the Knight should tell the first story?

2. Which features of the romance are evident in this tale?

3. How do Arcite and Palamon come to be imprisoned?

4. How is each man released from prison?

5. Why is Arcrite not recognized when he is employed in Emily's household?

6. How is it decided who will marry Emily?

7. What happens to prevent the man who won Emily's hand from marrying her?

8. What characteristics of chivalry are evident in the story?

9. What is the theme of The Knight's Tale?

10. From what sources did Chaucer borrow material for this tale?

Answers

1. He is the highest ranking member of the group.

2. The romantic features of this tale are: noble characters; ideal love; romantic past as setting; and trial by combat.

3. They are discovered, half-dead, on the battlefield at Thebes.

4. Arcite is freed by the intercession of a powerful friend. Palamon drugs the guard and escapes.

5. He has grown so thin and pale that he no longer looks like his former self.

6. The decision is made based on which knight's team wins the tournament staged by Theseus.

7. Arcite is thrown from his horse and mortally injured. He dies soon after.

8. The characteristics of chivalry in this tale include great attention to honorable behavior and trial by combat.

9. The theme of this tale is ideal love and chivalrous conduct.

10. Chaucer borrowed from: Boccaccio's *Teseide*, Boethius' *The Consolations of Philosophy*, and ancient myths.

Suggested Essay Topics

1. Explain the features of this tale which characterize it as a romance.

2. An "anachronism" is a literary "slip" in which the author inserts something into a work which could not have happened or which could not have existed at the time the work is set. Explain the anachronism in The Knight's Tale.

The Miller's Tale

Summary

The pilgrims congratulate the Knight on a wonderful story. The Host invites the Monk to tell another uplifting story, but the drunken Miller interrupts, insisting that he can match the Knight. The Host tries to stop the Miller, but the Miller will not be stopped. When he says he will tell a tale about a carpenter, the Reeve loudly objects; but it is to no avail. Chaucer warns the reader that the story may be coarse, but if the reader finds it offensive, he may choose another tale.

The Miller tells the story of a wealthy carpenter named John who has a very young and beautiful wife named Alison. Nicholas, a poor scholar of astrology, boards with John and Alison. Nicholas is young and lusty and covets the lovely Alison.

One day when John is away, Nicholas makes advances to Alison. She at first resists; however, Nicholas is persistent and Alison soon succumbs to his charms. She worries that her husband will kill her if he finds out, but Nicholas assures her that he will plan their time to make love so that the carpenter will never guess.

In the meantime, a lively parish clerk named Absalom also falls in love with Alison. Having an affair with her becomes his obsession and he makes a complete fool of himself in wooing her. Alison rebuffs him continually, but Absalom persists in his vain efforts to win her love.

Shortly after Alison and Nicholas fall in love, the carpenter goes away for the day again. The young lovers plan a way to complete their tryst. When John returns, Nicholas pretends to fall into an extended trance. When John finally succeeds in awakening him, Nicholas reveals that the stars and God have made known to him that within hours the world will again be destroyed by a great flood. Nicholas tells the carpenter that he, Alison, and Nicholas are to be saved if John will follow Nicholas' instructions.

John, who is incredibly gullible and desperate to save Alison, complies. As instructed, he suspends three large tubs from the beams in the ceiling and loads them with food and water. He puts in an axe to free the tubs when the water reaches ceiling level and chops an opening in the wall for the tubs to float through when the house fills up with water.

That night, Alison, John, and Nicholas climb into the tubs to sleep. Completely exhausted by his preparations, John falls into a dead sleep. The young lovers get out of the tubs and spend the night making love in the carpenter's bed.

That same night, Absalom determines to get Alison to at least kiss him. He stays awake all night and goes to her window when it is pitch-dark, just before dawn. Absalom begs Alison for a kiss and she finally agrees. However, instead of leaning her head out the window, Alison hangs her bare backside out, unbeknownst to Absalom. Absalom enthusiastically kisses her rear end. He is horrified and infuriated when he realizes he has been duped.

Determined to take revenge, Absalom rushes to the blacksmith's and borrows a hot poker. He runs back to the window and begs Alison for another kiss. This time, to further humiliate Absalom, Nicholas hangs his bare behind out the window, loudly breaking wind to complete the insult. Absalom applies the hot poker, nearly killing Nicholas with pain.

Nicholas begins to scream for water. His shouts waken John. Hearing only the word "water!" John assumes the flood has begun and chops the cords attaching the tubs to the ceiling. Everything crashes to the ground below and John is knocked unconscious in the fall.

Of course, all the neighbors are alerted by the racket and the chaos. They are hugely amused by the whole situation, and John is made a laughingstock in the community for the rest of his days. Both Nicholas and Absalom are humiliated, and the Miller concludes his tale, making the point that the gorgeous young Alison has made fools of them all.

Analysis

The Miller is coarse and common; the reader is warned that his tale will reflect his personality. The Miller and Reeve are rivals, possibly even acquainted on a personal basis. This tale is obviously written to contrast dramatically with the elevated tone of The Knight's Tale. The Miller's Tale is an example of the fabliau: set in contemporary times; peopled with everyday characters; dealing with one of Man's most basic functions, sexual appetite; concerned with cunning and folly; and meant to be funny.

These features contrast sharply with The Knight's Tale, which was a romance featuring a setting in the distant past, "aristocratic characters," concern with ideals and idealized love, a focus on the nature of good and evil, and which was meant to extol virtue.

The Miller's Tale is based on the traditional plot of a lovers' triangle, common in the French models with which Chaucer was familiar. It is also loaded with details which relate the tale to the medieval town of Oxford. For instance, Nicholas is the typical poor scholar who needs lodging; and John is the successful carpenter who has grown wealthy working on the cathedral being constructed nearby at Oseney. John's wealth enables him to have a house large enough to accommodate a boarder and to get a much younger woman to marry him. These factual details help make believable what is actually a fantastic story.

If this tale can be said to have a theme, it is probably the admonition at the beginning of the story: "…men should marry women of their own age, for youth and age are often at odds." John has married the young Alison mainly as an object; she is young, beautiful, and seductive—which makes him look good. He has acquired her to show her off, as a trophy of sorts. These are the wrong reasons for a man to marry, Chaucer seems to be saying; and John should have known better.

Study Questions

1. What are the main sources of humor in this story?
2. What does Chaucer seem to be saying about marriage?
3. What details make the tale seem realistic?
4. What basic human need motivates each of the characters?
5. Why is it appropriate for the Miller to tell this particular story?
6. Describe how The Miller's Tale qualifies as a fabliau.
7. What is the theme of the story?
8. What rivalry is set up before this tale is told?
9. How is the medieval fascination with astrology introduced into the story?
10. What traditional plot is present in The Miller's Tale?

Answers

1. The main sources of humor in this story consists of: tricking the carpenter into believing that the flood is coming; his elaborate preparations; the business with the bare bottoms; and the trickery turned upon Nicholas.
2. Older men should know better than to marry young girls.
3. Some details that make the tale seem realistic are: setting in Oxford and Oseney; business success of the carpenter; and the poor scholar.
4. Sexual appetite is the motivational human need in this tale.
5. The story is raucous and bawdy and coarse, like the Miller himself.
6. It is funny; it relies on trickery and deception; it deals with the basic sexual appetite; and its characters are everyday people.

7. The theme may be "youth and age are often at odds."

8. The rivalry between the Miller and the Reeve is set up before this tale is told.

9. Nicholas is a student of astrology and he uses the carpenter's belief in astrology as part of the hoax to get the carpenter to prepare for the flood.

10. The lovers' triangle, in this case two men desiring one woman, is the traditional plot line.

Suggested Essay Topics

1. Contrast The Knight's Tale with The Miller's Tale.

2. Fully describe the character Absalom.

The Reeve's Tale

Summary

All the pilgrims have laughed and enjoyed The Miller's Tale, but the favorable reception has angered the Reeve, who is himself an aging carpenter. He says that he, like all old men, is motivated by boasting, anger, lying, and covetousness. When the Host tells him to quit philosophizing and get on with his story, the Reeve promises to get even with the Miller.

Scornful Simkin is a wealthy miller who is armed to the teeth at all times and is very dishonest in his business dealings. No one dares accuse him, however, since he will immediately attack with one of the four weapons always on his person. Simkin has a wife with relatives among the nobility and a beautiful and desirable young daughter of marriageable age. They also have an infant still in the cradle.

One of the miller's most lucrative accounts is with the manager of the estates belonging to the college at Cambridge. One day, when he goes to collect the wheat and malt to be ground for the college, Simkin finds the steward terribly ill. He is delighted because it means he can cheat the college even more than usual.

The sick steward persuades two poor students to deliver the grain and to watch the miller to prevent his usual cheating. John and Allan, young and high-spirited, agree eagerly. They pretend interest in the milling process and position themselves to watch the miller's every move. Simkin, however, turns their horse loose and the young men must run away and try to capture their mount. The miller is then able to cheat unobserved.

When the young men return it is so late that they must spend the night. They offer to pay for a meal and a night's lodging. The miller goes to great lengths to fulfill his duties as a host. After eating a fine meal and getting drunk on ale, all of the characters retire to sleep in the same room. The miller and his wife are in their bed with the infant's cradle at the foot; the daughter is in her own bed; and John and Allan rest on an improvised cot.

Soon every member of the miller's family is loudly snoring and passing gas in their sleep. The young visitors realize they will not be getting a wink of sleep. Furthermore, they know the miller stole some of the grain in their absence. Allan decides he will sleep with the maiden daughter as compensation for his loss and discomfort.

As Allan is loudly making love to the girl, who is soon very cooperative, John determines that he, too, will retaliate. By the time the miller's wife gets up to relieve herself, John has moved the baby's cradle to the foot of his own bed. Missing the cradle at the foot of the marriage bed, the wife gropes in the dark until she locates the cradle. Satisfied, she climbs into bed with John. It is dark, so she eagerly responds to John's lovemaking thinking him her husband and delighted with his newfound energy.

At about dawn, Allan leaves the daughter's bed to return to his own. He avoids the bed with the cradle and climbs into bed with the miller whom he mistakes for his friend, John. Allan brags of his sexual conquest to the miller who immediately attacks him. Wrestling in the dark, the two fall on the miller's wife who thinks she is being attacked. She finds a stick and wacks her husband on the head, mistaking him for one of the students. Seeing the miller stunned and hurt, the students grab the advantage and beat him unconscious. They then escape back to Cambridge having made a complete fool of the deceitful miller.

Analysis

The rivalry and dislike between the Miller and the Reeve is again obvious. The Reeve's tale promises to be an exercise in one-up-manship that will outdo the Miller's tale.

Like the tale preceding, The Reeve's Tale is a fabliau, centering on sex and trickery and practical jokes. However, true to the character of the teller, this story is all about revenge. Chaucer used both French and Italian models for this parody; the plot would have been familiar to readers of his day.

What is most notable about this tale is the way it is used by the Reeve on the pilgrimage to get back at the Miller. First of all, the central character in the story is a dangerous and dishonest miller, presented in the most unflattering light possible. Secondly, this time it is the miller who is cuckolded and who suffers the further indignity of having his virgin daughter deflowered. In The Miller's Tale, the carpenter, John, is cuckolded; in The Reeve's Tale, it is the student, John, who cuckolds the miller. Even the physical description of the miller in the story matches the appearance and the character of the Miller on the pilgrimage. It becomes obvious that the hatred between the two men is more than just an occupational rivalry.

Study Questions

1. How does the miller, Simkin, parallel the Miller on the pilgrimage?

2. How is Simkin paid back by the clerics for his cheating?

3. What features of human nature are exaggerated in this tale?

4. What elements of the fabliau are present in The Reeve's Tale?

5. How does the Reeve pay the Miller back with this story?

6. What was the reaction of the other pilgrims to the tale told by the Miller?

7. Why was The Miller's Tale so offensive to the Reeve?

8. What qualities does the Reeve say characterize old men?

9. How does the infant in the cradle function in this story?

10. What "advantages" does Simkin's daughter have that make her a desirable bride?

Answers

1. The pilgrim Miller is loud and boastful; he is also dishonest. Simkin has the same characteristics.

2. One of them has sex with his wife while the other sleeps with his virgin daughter.

3. Sexual appetite, greed, and cunning are exaggerated in this tale.

4. The fabliau is represented by the following elements: sexual scenario; trickery; common people; and humor.

5. He makes the miller in the story out to be a fool who is completely tricked by two young men.

6. They all find it very funny.

7. The main character in the Miller's story was an aging carpenter who is made out to be a fool. The Reeve himself is aging and was formerly a carpenter. He takes the story as a personal insult, which is exactly how it was intended.

8. The Reeve says old men are characterized by boasting, anger, lying, and covetousness.

9. The infant in the cradle is used to confuse Simkin's wife and ultimately confuses one of the young men, as well.

10. The mother of the girl has a little bit of family background; the girl has a tiny bit of education; the father of the girl is wealthy; and she is a virgin.

Suggested Essay Topics

1. Explain how The Miller's Tale and The Reeve's Tale might be said to reveal a situation that medieval men really deplored and dreaded.

2. What might surprise the modern reader about the language surrounding sexual activity in The Miller's and The Reeve's Tales?

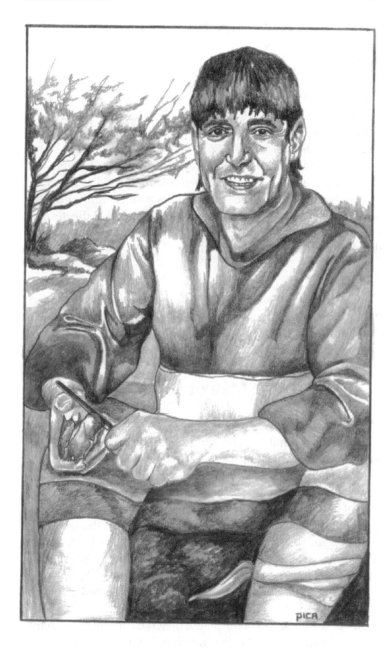

The Cook's Tale (Fragment)

Summary

The cook is mightily entertained by the story the Reeve told and wants to tell a funny story of his own. However, the Host reminds the Cook, who is named Hodge of Ware, that he owes the company a good tale since food he prepares so often makes travelers ill. Good-naturedly, the Cook begins his story.

Perkin the Reveler is apprenticed to a guild of food merchants. He is a wild and fun-loving youth, particularly fond of gambling and womanizing. Both vices require money which he lifts from his master's safe. One day, fed up, the master fires Perkin the Reveler. Perkin sends his personal belongings to the home of an equally devious friend...(Fragment concludes.)

Analysis

The Cook's Tale was probably intended to be another fabliau, but its unfinished state precludes analysis. It is interesting to note that another rivalry, this time between the Cook and the Host, seems to be surfacing.

The Man of Law's Tale

Summary

The Host reminds the company that the day is nearly one quarter over and they must hurry on with the telling of tales. He calls on the Man of Law to begin his story quickly. The worthy gentleman consents. He rambles along for a while, commenting that he cannot hope to imitate the well-known poet Chaucer in the quality of his speech, yet he will tell one in prose even though he be plainspoken. The teller then rambles on some more in an apparent sermon against poverty. It seems that his tale will somehow deal with this subject, but it certainly does not.

Part One: The Christian Emperor of Rome has a beautiful and extremely virtuous daughter named Constance whose reputation comes to the attention of the Sultan of Syria. Without even laying eyes on the lady, the Sultan falls madly in love with her and deter-

mines she must be his bride. He begins to negotiate for her hand, even promising to become Christian. The arrangements are finally concluded and Constance and the Sultan are married. In the meantime, the mother of the Sultan, horrified that her son is so willing to renounce his Muslim faith, has plotted against the alliance.

Part Two: Shortly after the marriage, the Sultan's mother gives a banquet to honor the newlyweds. Once all the guests are seated, her henchmen assassinate all who assisted in the marriage and embraced the Christian faith, including her own son, the Sultan.

Only Constance is spared, but is placed on a rudderless ship to float aimlessly over all the seas until she eventually suffers some terrible death. The Mother of Christ intervenes in behalf of Constance and spares her life. The ship lands in Britain.

Constance is befriended by the King's warden and his wife. Both come to love her virtuous and sweet nature. Hermengild, the warden's wife, is so impressed by Constance's piety that she becomes a secret Christian.

A young knight in the area falls in love with Constance. When his efforts to seduce her fail, he seeks revenge by framing Constance for the murder of Hermingild which he has actually committed. While the warden was away, Hermengild and Constance slept in the same bed. The wicked young knight sneaked into the bedchamber, slit Hermengild's throat, covered Constance with the blood, and placed the bloody weapon in Constance's hand.

When the warden returns and comes upon the scene, he can only conclude that Constance is the murderer. However, the cruelty of the act is so out of character for Constance the warden takes her to King Aella to be judged. All those who testify speak of her virtue and hold her to be incapable of the crime, except for the knight, who finally swears on the Bible that Constance is guilty. The Lord knocks him down as he gives this false witness and the voice of God is heard declaring Constance innocent. This miracle brings about the conversion of all present. King Aella has the evil knight executed and Constance is pardoned.

Naturally, Aella also soon falls in love with Constance and marries her. She becomes pregnant, but just as she is about to deliver, Aella is called away to fight the Scots. Constance is safely delivered of a beautiful boy and immediately sends a messenger to King Aella with the good news.

Unfortunately, the messenger stops first at the palace of the king's mother who hates Constance. She gets the messenger drunk and substitutes a false letter that says Constance has given birth to a monster and accuses Constance of being a witch. When Aella receives this letter he is terribly sad, but sends a reply stating that he accepts the will of God and hopes for a more normal child the next time.

On the return trip, the messenger stops again at the palace of the king's mother. Again he falls into a drunken slumber, and again, the wicked mother-in-law substitutes a false letter for the real one. The counterfeit letter orders the warden to put Constance and the baby in the same ship in which Constance had arrived and to put that ship again out to sea.

When the letter arrives, the brokenhearted warden has no choice but to obey his king. Amid great and terrible sorrow, Constance and the baby leave Britain on the rudderless ship.

Part Three: When King Aella returns home, he is dumbfounded at the state of affairs he finds. Under torture, the messenger reveals the plot. Both he and the king's mother are executed, but the king mourns perpetually for his lost wife and child.

After five years and one false landing, Constance is intercepted by a Roman senator who, coincidentally, is just returning to Rome after punishing the Syrians for their treachery to her. Constance remains anonymous, but does take up lodging with the senator and his wife. Like nearly everyone else who has known her, this couple, their household, and their friends come to love the wonderful guest and to admire her greatly.

In the meantime, King Aella feels compelled to go to Rome to repent for killing his mother. While in Rome, he becomes acquainted with the Senator. The senator is invited to a banquet given by King Aella and takes Contance's son, Maurice, with him. When Aella perceives the resemblance of Maurice to Constance and hears the story of the boy's mother, he begins to wonder if he has found his lost wife and child.

Within a few days, Aella goes to the senator's home where he and Constance are finally reunited. When all is finally understood, they embrace madly and kiss hundreds of times.

Aella then invites Constance's father, who is also ignorant of her identity, to dine with them. The Emperor, her father, is overjoyed to see Constance again. He is also pleased to meet her husband and son. After this episode, Aella, Constance, and Maurice return to England to a happy, peaceful life, but after a year, Aella dies. Constance and Maurice return to Rome. When the Emperor dies, Maurice is named Emperor of Rome, and Constance continues in virtue and piety all the rest of her days.

Analysis

In the prologue to this tale, there is a reference to stories Chaucer has already published in *The Legend of Good Women.* This leads to commentary about the nature of a story as something told rather than as something that happened. It also presents the medieval notion that stories are something like a commodity which can be used up. In other words, there is a limited number of plots and most of the good stories have already been told. Actually, Chaucer will contradict this notion in *The Canterbury Tales* by rearranging incidents and characters to create vigorously new stories.

Because several elements of this prologue do not seem to fit what follows, many critics believe that the Man of Law was originally intended to be the first of the travellers to tell his story. This would account for the very literary nature of the prologue. That Chaucer changed his mind sometime after writing the prologue accounts for the incongruity between the introduction and the story that follows.

The extreme wordiness and the rambling nature of the Man of Law's introduction certainly do fit the character who is described in the General Prologue as a very pompous and successful lawyer. It would be natural for such a man to use elaborate language and to talk in circles.

By this time, the reader has noticed that many of *The Canterbury Tales* relate to themes examining the nature of love and the nature of marriage. This story of Constance continues in that vein, extolling the virtues of the good wife through extreme tribulation. Unlike the women in the fabliau tales, all of whom are sexually "easy," Constance is chaste and pure. The men who try to steal her virtue are all killed.

The religious overtones with the direct intervention of the Virgin Mary and of God Himself in Constance's behalf give the story elements of the popular saints' lives widely told in Chaucer's day. The tale also has features of romance, folktale, and tragedy. Like many Greek myths, The Man of Law's Tale uses the motifs of sea travel, loss, and recognition scenes. There are also numerous Latin references drawn from the Bible and other classical sources. That all of these elements are united successfully to produce an excellent story is evidence both of Chaucer's enormous personal scholarship and of his skill as a storyteller.

The structure of The Man of Law's Tale is worth noting. First, the author employs a good deal of repetition: voyages, treachery, evil mothers-in-law, banquets, and supernatural interventions are all repeated in Constance's life story. Secondly, the constant divine interest in the character and the frequency of His intervention exploit the theological notion that persistence in faith is ultimately rewarded with joy. This same theme is actually an underlying structure of the tale. Constance moves several times through unbearable suffering to peace and joy. Yet each time she arrives at a state of happiness, that state is quickly destroyed by evil until the very end when Constance is reunited with her father, a parallel to the reunion of Man with God at the end of life. The strong theological theme is characteristic of the time when narratives were often used to drive home a moral lesson.

Study Questions

1. What concession does the Sultan of Syria make in order to obtain the hand of Constance in marriage?

2. How does Constance end up a widow landing on the coast of Britain?

3. How does Constance come to wed King Aella?

4. What type of wife is Constance intended to represent?

5. How does this contrast with the wives in the preceding stories?

6. List the types of narratives that Chaucer drew on to create this tale.

7. What device is employed extensively in the structure of the tale?

8. Describe the underlying theological theme of The Man of Law's Tale.

9. Describe the events that lead Constance from joy to despair to joy and so on.

10. State the moral of this tale.

Answers

1. He agrees to become a Christian.

2. The Sultan is murdered by his mother who also casts Constance off in a rudderless ship.

3. She is introduced to him when she is accused of a murder. The witnesses in her favor and divine intervention convince King Aella of her innocence and virtue. He soon comes to love her and they are wed.

4. The virtuous wife who endures all tribulations and trials.

5. Those women were sexually very lax while Constance is chaste and virtuous.

6. Saints' lives; folktale; romance; myth; tragedy; and biblical text are the types of narratives Chaucer drew on for this tale.

7. Repetition is employed extensively.

8. Persistence in faith is ultimately rewarded with joy.

9. Constance's life was at first a joy with her parents. She found despair when the Sultan was murdered and she was set out to sea. She again found joy when she married King Aella and they had a son. She thought that Aella had rejected her and their son because of the mother-in-law's intervention. She was then set out to sea once again causing her distress. She was then rescued and reunited with her father and, later, Aella. However, Aella died a mere year later. She found peace again at the end when she was reunited with her father and her son Maurice inherited the throne.

10. Virtue is always rewarded or faith will ultimately triumph.

Suggested Essay Topics

1. Describe what commentary about marriage seems to be made through this tale.

2. Name one element of the story that is drawn from each of the narrative types that Chaucer utilized for this tale.

The Shipman's Tale

Summary

The Host invites the Parson to tell his story next. When the Parson admonishes the Host for his drunkenness, the Host jokingly accuses the Parson of being a prude, and maybe even a heretic. Their interchange is rudely interrupted by the Shipman who says he will tell a jolly tale with no hint of preaching in it.

His tale begins with a very successful merchant who lived at St. Denis with his very beautiful wife, a woman excessively fond of entertaining and dressing herself to be admired. To accommodate her, the merchant kept a very fine house which was always filled with visitors. Frequently among them was a monk called Don John, a handsome man of 30. He and the merchant had become such close friends that they referred to themselves as cousins.

On the occasion being described, the monk comes to visit just as the merchant is preparing to leave on a buying trip. The merchant takes an inventory of his assets while the monk recites his prayer walking in the garden. The beautiful wife approaches the monk and unburdens herself of all her marital troubles. She claims that her husband is miserly and that she needs 100 pounds to purchase a new dress. Don John agrees to lend her the money. He kisses and caresses her. It is understood that repayment will be made in sexual favors.

When the merchant emerges from his counting house, Don John borrows from him the 100 pounds, gladly loaned him by his "cousin." The monk promises to repay quickly and admonishes the merchant to behave sensibly while away.

The following Sunday, with the merchant safely out of town, the monk gives the money to the wife. They agree that a night in bed together will be ample repayment of the loan and make merry all that night in the absence of the husband.

When the merchant returns, his wife joyfully welcomes him home. However, the merchant has to leave for Paris right away as he has acquired some debt making his purchases and needs to borrow some money.

In Paris, the merchant calls on Don John for the sake of their friendship. The monk gives a banquet in his honor and inquires about the business trip. The merchant admits his debt and Don John remarks that he is glad to have already repaid the loan. He claims to have left the 100 pounds on a bench with the merchant's wife, who had given him a verbal receipt for the gold.

Once the merchant borrows all he needs, he returns home in high good humor. He and his wife delightedly make love all night. However, on the morning, the merchant asks her about the gold left by the monk.

Thinking quickly, the wife says she has spent the money on clothes and that her husband must be content with her repaying him day by day as people admire her beauty. That admiration will do him credit which will constitute repayment. She further assures him that her continued enthusiasm for their lovemaking will recompense him for the gold.

The merchant sees immediately that he is beaten. Ruefully, he tells his adorable wife not to be so careless with his money in the future. There the story ends.

Analysis

The Shipman is clearly bored with morality. He wants nothing of a sermonizing nature in his tale; its only purpose is to entertain. His tale is another example of fabliau, with its emphasis on trickery and sex. Like many of the other tales, this one centers on a theme of marriage. The beautiful wife in this story manages both her husband and Don John by bestowing her sexual favors with enthusiasm to achieve her own ends.

Because so much of this story is presented from a female perspective, and because the Wife of Bath was said to be so skilled in all the arts of love, many critics believe that Chaucer originally intended for this tale to be told by the earthy Wife of Bath. However, The Shipman is a very worldly and a very nonreligious man, thus having him tell the story is not out of keeping with his character as it is described in the General Prologue.

Study Questions

1. How does the wife in the story obtain the money she needs for her new dress?

2. How is Don John's loan actually repaid and by whom?

3. Does the merchant learn of the arrangement between his wife and Don John?

4. What elements of the fabliau are obvious in this tale?

5. What does the author seem to be saying about marriage?

6. What rationale does the wife use to convince the husband that she really must be well-dressed?

7. Does the husband, who is a merchant, appear to be miserly or just careful?

8. What makes the monk Don John unattractive as a person?

9. How does the merchant in this story seem to parallel the pilgrim Merchant?

10. Why is this tale suited to the Shipman? (refer to General Prologue)

Answers

1. She borrows it from the monk, Don John.

2. The wife spends the night making love to Don John. That is the repayment.

3. The merchant never learns nor suspects the arrangement.

4. Infidelity; the trickery of the husband; and the sexual nature of the tale are the obvious fabliau elements here.

5. Wives cannot be trusted where other men and finery are involved.

6. She tells him that her attractiveness reflects well on him.

7. He is careful.

8. He is a very conniving and disloyal friend to the merchant. He also betrays his vows as a monk.

9. The Merchant on the pilgrimage is said to be a gambler and risk-taker. The merchant in the tale has risked all by purchasing more merchandise than he can pay for on the speculation that it will sell well and earn him a profit.

10. The Shipman has travelled all over and is familiar with many foreign ports, such as St. Denis where this story is set. He is unscrupulous just like the monk who cuckolds the merchant. He wants no moralizing or preaching so his characters seem to have no consciences.

Suggested Essay Topics

1. Of the six tales told thus far, including the Cook's fragment, four have been fabliaux. What is the significance of the large number of fabliaux?

2. Discuss the two contrasting views of women that are represented in the tales so far.

The Prioress's Tale

Summary

After jesting rather coarsely about the monk in the Shipman's Tale—and monks in general—the Host switches to a tone of exaggerated politeness in inviting the Prioress to tell her tale.

A very young schoolboy learns a difficult Latin hymn of praise to the Virgin Mary because of his deep devotion to her. Every day, on the way to school and on the way home, he passes through the Jewish ghetto of the town singing the hymn.

Taking his singing as a direct insult, a group of wicked Jews has an assassin slit the boy's throat. The child's widowed mother searches for him everywhere. She finally discovers his poor little body on a dung heap. Miraculously, the child is still singing his hymn.

The Christians of the town bear his body to the monastery for burial, awed by the miracle of the child's continued singing. The boy, still able to speak, reveals to the abbot that the Virgin Mary has placed a miraculous kernel on his tongue which enables him to hold to life and continue his song. Profoundly affected, the Abbott removes the kernel and the child's pure spirit ascends to heaven. All the Christians are confirmed in their faith and the wicked Jews are tortured and killed.

Analysis

True to her perfectionist, sentimental nature, the Prioress begins with a long apologetic prayer to the Virgin Mary. Her story of the martyred child resembles popular saints' stories of the day. It has a very preachy and morbid tone.

Though they appear to the modern reader as very negative aspects of this story, her reverence for chastity and her harsh judgment of the Jews are both reflections of common medieval Catholic beliefs. The violent nature of the events in the story seem to be in contradiction to a personality as sensitive as the Prioress's is supposed to be, suggesting that she may be much tougher than she wishes to reveal. She is, after all, in a position of great authority over others.

Study Questions

1. Who is the central character in the story?
2. What is his special mark of devotion to the Virgin Mary?
3. Why do the Jews in the story hate the boy so much?
4. Describe the grim nature of the boy's murder.
5. What miraculous circumstance attends the finding of the murdered boy?
6. How is the abbot able to release the boy's soul?
7. How do the Catholics interpret the child's amazing singing?
8. How does the modern reader account for the treatment of the Jews in this tale?
9. Why is it appropriate that this tale should be told by the Prioress?
10. What happens to the Jews in the tale?

Answers

1. The protagonist is a very young schoolboy.

2. He sings a hymn to the Blessed Virgin.

3. He sings his song each day passing through the Jewish ghetto of the town. They are insulted by the nature of his song.

4. His throat is slit and his body is thrown on a dung heap.

5. When his body is found, the boy is still singing and able to communicate.

6. The Virgin Mary has placed a kernel on the boy's tongue. When the abbot removes it, the boy's soul is released.

7. The singing represents a miracle.

8. Medieval Catholics despised and mistreated Jews.

9. The Prioress is of an overly sensitive and sentimental nature; the story is very sentimental.

10. The Jews are tortured and killed.

Suggested Essay Topics

1. Explain aspects of the story which may be offensive to modern readers.

2. What aspects of the story may reveal a hidden quality in the Prioress?

The Tale of Sir Thopas

Summary

After the sobering miracle story, the Host calls on the Narrator to give a lively, amusing story. (The Host fancies himself something of a literary critic; apparently, the pilgrim Narrator's genial nature has led Harry Bailley to believe that the Narrator will know some excellent tales.) Apologetically, with tongue in cheek, the Narrator says he knows only one old story in rhyme-doggerel. (Rhyme-doggerel was a sing-song form of poetry associated with low-class humor.)

The First Fit: Sir Thopas, in all his youthful perfection and vanity, is closely described. One day, Sir Thopas rides out to hunt and falls into a fit of "love-longing." He finds no woman worthy to be the object of his love. Feeling it to be the obvious decision, Sir Thopas decides to seek an elf queen to love.

Sir Thopas rides hard in his search and ends up in the kingdom of the Queen of Fairies. He is arrested by an enormous giant who tells Sir Thopas to leave immediately or he will kill Sir Thopas' horse. Sir Thopas makes an appointment with the giant for 9:00 the next morning at which time he intends to fight and slay the giant.

The giant begins to pelt Sir Thopas with stones from his enormous sling-shot, but the young knight, of course, manages to escape. He orders his servants to prepare a feast and entertainment for him to strengthen him this night before his battle. He tells them that he must fight a giant with three heads for the love of someone whom he has never seen. The next morning, Sir Thopas dons enough armor to weight a man into the ground and rides off to slay the giant.

The Second Fit: As the Narrator begins reciting the second part of his story, the Host interrupts, proclaiming the tale very base, common and unamusing, and a waste of time. Chaucer defends himself, saying that although his version of the story may not be to the Host's liking, it is still a good story. The Host insists that he leave off the terrible rhyme. The Narrator says he will do so and will tell a moral tale in prose. He tells the Host not to interrupt him again.

The Narrator now tells a long, long tale about Melibeus, a nobleman who wants to take revenge against enemies who have hurt his wife and daughter. His wife, Prudence, however, persuades Melibeus to consult his friends before exacting revenge. However, the friends give conflicting advice and Melibeus remains determined to go to war.

Prudence then persuades Melibeus to allow her to meet in secret conference with his enemies. These men are convinced by Prudence to admit their wrong and to submit to judgment by her relatives. The relatives rule for peace. Melibeus decides to accept their verdict and forgive his enemies.

Analysis

Chaucer's two stories are actually a joke on the Host with his impossible pretensions to being a literary critic. The Tale of Sir Thopas, which Harry Bailley totally rejects, is actually a brilliant parody of the popular courtly romances. Sir Thopas, vain and empty-headed, is going off to slay a dragon in response to his lovelonging and not in defense of any ladylove. He is behaving in exaggerated knightly fashion, but the absence of any ideals makes him completely ludicrous.

The literal-minded Host cannot see this; he is merely disgusted by the use of such a low form of versification for what is supposed to be a courtly story. Harry is not disappointed, however, by the narrator's long, ponderous telling of a rather boring and highly moralistic story. Harry fully approves when the Narrator deliberately loads the narrative with proverbs, maxims, clichés, and literary allusions, tripling its length in the process. To the Host, this makes the story of Melibeus properly serious. The Narrator's joke escapes him completely.

Study Questions

1. What elements of the romance are found in the story of Sir Thopas?

2. What leads the reader to understand that the story is a parody?

3. On what ancient form of literature is the Tale of Melibeus based?

4. What causes Harry Bailley to disapprove of The Tale of Sir Thopas?

5. Why does he approve of the Tale of Melibeus?

6. What kind of a wife is Prudence in the story of Melibeus?

7. Explain how The Tale of Sir Thopas is a joke on the Host.

8. In what way does the story of Melibeus complete the joke?

9. What does the Narrator call the divisions in The Tale of Sir Thopas?

10. What is rhyme-doggerel?

Answers

1. Romance is represented in this tale by a gallant knight off on a quest and combat for love.

2. Everything is exaggerated, such as the knightly qualities of Sir Thopas. Also, the story is divided into "fits" instead of sections or parts. The encounter with the giant is ridiculous.

3. The Tale of Melibeus is based upon ancient Greek and Roman myths.

4. It is in rhyme-doggerel, the base jargon of the streets, and low verse. This is not suited for a courtly tale, in the Host's opinion.

5. It is sober, serious, and long.

6. Prudence is wise and patient.

7. The main character, the situation and the form are ridiculous and wonderful, but the Host cannot see this. He is far too literal-minded.

8. It is of terrible quality; long, boring, and trite, but the Host does not see this, either. He judges it excellent.

9. He calls them "fits."

10. A low, base form of poetry with forced rhyme.

Suggested Essay Topics

1. Describe the Host as he has revealed himself so far in the dialogues.

2. Explain the humor, point by point, in the Tale of Sir Thopas.

The Monk's Tale

Summary

The Host comments that he wishes his own wife were as patient as Prudence in the Tale of Melibeus. He describes Goodlief, his wife, as ill-tempered in the extreme and big and brawny into the bargain. In short, Harry reveals that he is henpecked.

The Host then turns the company's attention to the Monk, whom he abuses at length, supposedly in jest. Harry comments on the Monk's well-fed and sturdy appearance, remarks that he would make a fine breeder, and adds that if the Host had his way, all the monks and priests would have wives and beget fine children. Harry feels that the Church is taking all the best men and leaving only weaklings among the laity who are fathering inferior offspring.

The Monk bears all this taunting and disrespect patiently. As if to defend the seriousness of his commitment to the religious life, he vows to tell some tragedies which he defines as stories relating to persons of high station and prosperity who fall from power into misery and poverty.

The Monk's Tale turns out to be a lengthy list of noble historical, biblical, and mythological characters who suffered misfortune. Each recitation is very short and is intended to be a warning against trusting in the permanence of luck or prosperity. The characters the Monk deals with are: Lucifer, Adam, Samson, Hercules, Nebuchadnezzar, Belshazzar, Zenobia, King Pedro of Spain, King Peter of Cyprus, Barnabo of Lombardy, Count Ugolino of Pisa, Nero, Holofernes, Antiochus, Alexander, Julius Caesar, and Croesus.

Analysis

The Host's scorn for the clergy is evident in this prologue. He is not really eager to increase the population by having the clergy marry; he is rather implying that all monks are lecherous scoundrels.

The Monk's Tale (actually 17 short recitations) contradicts the Host's lewd jests. It is very serious and sorrowful and gives a typical clerical admonition that Man must not trust fame and fortune, for they are fleeting and temporal.

Study Questions

1. What kind of a wife does the Host have?

2. How does the description of Harry Bailley's married state fit in with the theme of many of the tales?

3. What is the Host's opinion of the clergy?

4. How does the Monk respond to the teasing of the Host?

5. What is the theme of The Monk's Tale?

6. From what sources are the examples drawn?

7. The Monk's Tale is not actually a story. What is it?

8. List three of the 17 notable figures described in this section.

9. Against what is the Monk warning the listeners?

10. Why must the listeners not trust in these things?

Answers

1. She is ill-tempered; she is big and strong.

2. Harry's wife is in control; he is very anxious to please her. This situation is repeated often in the tales, particularly in The Wife of Bath's Tale.

3. The Host sees them as lecherous and dishonest. He also feels that many of the best potential fathers are joining the Church.

4. The Monk responds patiently; he does not seem upset.

5. The theme of the tale centers on tragedies that have befallen great figures.

6. The Monk uses sources from history, the Bible, and myths as the basis for what he says.

7. It is a long recitation giving examples of the tragedies mentioned.

8. All 17 notable figures are noted in the summary on the previous page.

9. He warns against trusting in fame and fortune.

10. They are fleeting; they will last only a short time.

Suggested Essay Topics

1. What does the Monk's decision to give a long moral recitation rather than tell a tale reveal about his character—especially in view of his outwardly patient response to the Host?

2. Taking one of the historical figures the Monk mentions in his recitation, discuss how that person specifically ties in to the Monk's theme (you cannot trust fame and fortune).

The Nun's Priest's Tale

Summary

The Knight interrupts the listing of tragedies by the Monk, saying that such grim recitals are making everyone sad. The Host immediately agrees, commenting that the long narration has almost put everyone to sleep. He begs the Monk to tell them something different. When the Monk declines, Harry calls upon the Nun's Priest to tell a happy story. The Priest laughingly agrees, seeing that the clever Monk has revenged himself on Harry Bailley by nearly boring him to death.

He begins his tale about a poor old widow who owns a remarkable rooster named Chanticleer. For crowing exactly on time he has no equal, and the splendor of his colored feathers and his coral comb is amazing. Chanticleer has seven hens, all of whom are his wives and sisters, but the one he loves the most is called Demoiselle Partlet.

One day at dawn, Partlet hears Chanticleer moaning strangely. When she inquires in alarm about this clamor, Chanticleer reveals that he has had a strange and terrifying dream. In the dream, a yellow-red beast with black-tipped ears and tail grabbed him and intended to kill him. Partlet scorns Chanticleer, saying it is only a dream and he is truly a coward to be frightened by it. She recommends he find herbs to purge his system; she is convinced nightmares are no more than a symptom of indigestion.

Chanticleer then defends his fear by recounting several stories in which very important and learned men were warned of impending disaster in their dreams. Those who heeded the warnings, taking the dreams seriously, were saved; but those who ignored the warning perished. Therefore, he concludes, he has every right to take the dream seriously. Furthermore, he tells Partlet that he puts no stock in laxatives. Then Chanticleer resorts to his usual cheerfulness and amorousness with his beloved. He appears to forget all about the dream.

Unknown to the family of fowls, that same night when Chanticleer was having his horrible nightmare, a sly yellow-red fox with black-tipped ears and tail had crept into the yard and is lying low among the herbs, waiting for his chance to attack Chanticleer. As the rooster is walking in the yard, he spies the fox and almost has a fit he is so frightened.

The fox tells Chanticleer not to be afraid, for he has come to listen to Chanticleer sing his remarkable songs. He flatters Chanticleer so lavishly that the vain fellow is completely disarmed and begins to crow. While the rooster is thus distracted, Sir Russell, the fox, snatches the bird in his mouth and begins to run, intending to kill and eat Chanticleer.

Partlet and the other hens begin to shriek madly, raising such a din that the widow, her children, the dogs, and then the entire neighborhood begin to chase the fox. All the barnyard animals run around, scream, and add to the chaos.

When Sir Russell reaches the edge of the forest, he stops a moment to rest. At this point, the clever Chanticleer says that the fox should just tell the pursuing crowd to give up since the marvelous fox is so much faster at running than they are. It is obvious Sir Russell cannot be overtaken. The proud fox opens his mouth to utter the boast suggested by the rooster, and Chanticleer flies out of his mouth up into a tree beyond the fox's reach.

The fox again tries to trick Chanticleer by flattery, but the rooster has learned his lesson. He refuses to succumb again to the fox's flattery and deception. Sir Russell skulks away and Chanticleer is saved.

The Host enthusiastically congratulates the priest on an excellent tale, adding comments about the priest's surprising vigor and manliness to the commentary.

Analysis

The Host is greatly relieved when the Monk is prevented by the Knight from recounting any more of his ponderous recital. When the Priest agrees to tell a merry tale, the entire company is delighted.

The Nun's Priest's Tale of Chanticleer is one of the finest beast fables in the English language. In this format, beasts personify humans and exaggerate Man's characteristics, usually for the purpose of teaching a lesson. The characters, as in this case with Chanticleer, often make use of classical learning to solidify their moral instruction.

Chaucer probably based this story on the French *Roman de Renart* and the German Reinhart Fuchs; but, as was his custom, the author of *The Canterbury Tales* dramatically altered the plots. In the European models, the rooster is a self-centered idiot who repeatedly refused to listen to warnings. As the reader has observed, Chaucer's Chanticleer, although somewhat vain, is a victim of love. He overrides his own better judgment and goes into the yard to please Partlet whom he loves very dearly. It is, therefore, for love of Partlet that Chanticleer becomes the fox's victim.

The obvious moral lesson of the foolishness of succumbing to empty flattery diverts attention from a more subtle warning to beware the advice of women. This was a popular medieval theme. Woman, the original seductress, was the source of much of Man's sinfulness. As the weaker and less intellectually endowed of the two sexes, Woman was not a reliable counselor. This theme is in deliberate stark contrast to the Tale of Melibeus, whose central figure, Prudence the wise wife, counsels patience and prevents a war.

The tale is suitable to the teller when one considers the position of the Nun's Priest. He is the servant of the Prioress who appears to be silly and sentimental. His work forces him to live in a community of women drawn by her to the convent; it is likely that they are as silly as their mistress, in which case, the Priest would naturally have a somewhat low opinion of women.

In the Epilogue to the tale, the Host is once again in high good humor and full of bawdy teasing for the Priest. He next invites the Wife of Bath to tell her story.

Study Questions

1. In what genre is The Nun's Priest's Tale written?

2. How do the rooster and the hens and the fox reflect the typical format of this genre?

3. How has Chaucer altered the traditional plot of this old tale?

4. What is the obvious moral theme?

5. What is the more subtle theme of the story?

6. What is Chanticleer's great fault?

7. What is the redeeming quality that prevents his destruction?

8. What commentary about the nature of women is inserted in this tale?

9. What brings an end to the long list of tragedies the Monk was recounting?

10. How has the Monk revenged himself on Harry Bailley?

Answers

1. It is written as a beast fable.

2. They are animals who have been given human characteristics, situations, and problems.

3. In the models, Chanticleer is totally vain and without wisdom; in Chaucer's version, the rooster is a victim of love and learns from his mistake.

4. Do not listen to or act upon flattery.

5. Beware the advice of women.

6. He is vain.

7. He learns from his mistake and is not victimized a second time.

8. Women are the source of sin and are not to be trusted as advisors.

9. The Knight interrupts and says the audience has had enough and is growing depressed.

10. He has nearly bored the Host to death.

Suggested Essay Topics

1. By relating the theme of women to the Nun's Priest, explain why it is appropriate that he tell this tale.

2. Explain how The Nun's Priest's Tale fits the requirements for a beast fable.

The Wife of Bath's Tale

Summary

The Wife of Bath tells the travelers that she has buried five husbands and has lived in the married state since she was 12 years old. Furthermore, she is now looking for her sixth husband. For these reasons, she considers herself an expert on the subject of matrimony.

Before telling her story, the Wife feels compelled to defend her numerous marriages. In a lengthy monologue, she counters the religious arguments against multiple marriages. For instance, she says, although God and St. Paul recommend chastity as a perfect state, neither of them expressly forbid marriage. Since she is not perfect and has no desire to be, she personally prefers being married as she has an enormous appetite for sexual activity. In any case, she says, God calls people to Him in many ways: He calls her to marriage.

Continuing the argument, the Wife adds that God would not have given men and women sexual organs if He did not intend for them to be used. The good Wife has learned to use her sexual organs to their best advantage, which is, in her opinion, as instruments with which to control her husbands.

The Pardoner interrupts to say that he was about to marry, but now that he has listened to the Wife of Bath, he is not so sure he wants to volunteer to be controlled in the way she is describing. The Wife tells him to keep listening.

Next, this lively narrator launches into her personal philosophy of marriage. It is, in a nutshell, that the wife must control the husband if the marriage is to succeed. She details how the woman acquires and keeps control. The Wife knows this because three of her husbands were rich, old, and easy to control, which constitute the perfect characteristics for husbands in her opinion. She is sure her management of them made all of these men happy.

Specifically, she tells the travelers, she always made it a practice to accuse the men constantly of infidelity, deception, and criticism. The husbands, therefore, were continually occupied defending themselves and proving the Wife mistaken by giving her their attention, their devotion, and many, many gifts. Their fortunes she had wisely secured before even marrying them.

While the men she married were thus absorbed in proving their devotion, the Wife of Bath could, and did, dally with whomever she pleased. If the Wife's gadding about at night and keeping company with a handsome young attendant became a subject for comment by the husband, she would merely turn the tables on him. She would declare that spying on the husband as he went "wenching" at night necessitated her absences and her bodyguard.

The merry Wife admits that she has grown fond of drinking as she has aged, finding it a stimulus to her sexual nature and making her less able to resist the advances of men. She mourns the loss of her youth but is still determined to be happy.

Next in this extremely long prologue, she tells about her fourth husband who was a reveller and had a mistress, which made her very jealous. She repaid him by making him aware of how attractive she was to other men. This, in turn, made him constantly jealous of her. Yet, the Wife also confides that all the while she was married to the fourth husband, she was flirting with Jenkin, a young former cleric who had been a scholar at Oxford. According to the Wife, she convinced Jenkin that he had enchanted her and that if she were free, she would marry him.

Jenkin evidently believed the lady, for when they buried the fourth husband, he walked behind the bier and made eyes at the Wife. The good widow did not weep too much realizing that she had already cemented her fifth marriage. This though Jenkin was 20 and she was 40.

In the fifth marriage, however, the Wife admits she made the terrible mistake of giving Jenkin control, including all the lands and properties she had inherited from the previous husbands. As a consequence, Jenkin would not do anything she wanted. Furthermore, and what was worse, Jenkin actually tried to control her. He forbade her to go visiting and preached at her constantly, quoting from segments about bad wives from learned books.

Finally, one night when he was reading to her about the troubles famous men had had with their wives, the Wife of Bath grew so exasperated with Jenkin that she tore three pages from the book and punched him in the cheek. He retaliated by hitting her so hard that she fell back, apparently unconscious. Terrified that he had killed her, and overwhelmed with relief when her mock

unconsciousness disappeared, Jenkin gave the Wife back control
of their marriage and they lived happily until he died.

The Friar is greatly amused by this narration, but he comments
that it was certainly a very long introduction to her story. Jumping
to the Wife's defense, the Summoner insults the Friar, the Friar
retaliates. The Host quiets the feuding clergymen and the Wife of
Bath finally tells her story.

In the days of King Arthur, a young knight rides out from the
court one day, and when he spies a beautiful and solitary maiden,
he ravishes her. The girl's outraged family appeals to Arthur for
justice, and Arthur condemns the youth to death.

However, the Queen and her ladies take pity on the tragic
young knight and persuade Arthur to leave the youth to their
judgment. The Queen commands the youth to spend a year
traveling all across the country interviewing women. At the end of
the year, he is to return to court and be able to tell the Queen what
it is that women most desire. If he cannot provide the correct
response, he will forfeit his life.

After a year of searching for this knowledge, the young knight
has received so many different answers that he despairs of
surviving his trial. As he sadly and reluctantly begins his journey
back to the court, he happens upon an exceedingly ugly old
woman. When he tells her of his sad state, the old woman
promises to give him the answer he is seeking if he will swear to
grant her anything she wishes. The young knight eagerly gives his
word in exchange for which the hag confides to him the proper
answer to the question proposed by the Queen.

The old woman accompanies the youth back to the court.
When they are ushered into the presence of the Queen, she asks if
he has learned what it is that women most desire. He gives her the
answer supplied by the ancient woman; that women wish to have
complete control of their husbands, their love affairs, and to be
the master of their men.

When this turns out to be the correct response, the old hag
claims her wish. She wants the handsome young knight to marry
her. Horrified, he begs her to change her mind, but she refuses.

Sad and appalled at what he is doing, the young man marries
the old woman; but when he lies with her on the wedding night,

he can feel no passion. When she asks him why he is such a reluctant lover, he tells her it is because she is so poor, old, and ugly.

Getting his attention immediately, the old hag says she can change her form in three days time. However, she lectures eloquently about the mistakenness of judging people by their appearance. She tells him to decide, after reflecting on the wisdom of all she has said, whether he wants her to remain ugly and old, yet a humble and faithful wife; or whether he would have her become young and lovely, but probably an unreliable and troublesome wife.

The young husband ruefully chooses to have the old woman remain as she is, whereupon she rewards him by remaining humble and faithful, at the same time becoming young and beautiful. Thus, the knight's good judgment is rewarded and the two then live happily together from that moment on.

Interjecting herself again, the Wife of Bath closes her tale with a prayer that Jesus send women handsome and virile husbands together with the strength to outlive them. She curses men who will not be ruled by their wives and says Amen.

Analysis

In her lengthy introduction, the Wife of Bath reveals a great deal about herself. She is unquestionably a feminist: mercenary, amorous, and aggressive in the bargain. Chaucer has made her intelligent as well, quite adept at argumentation.

The Wife's policy in marriage is to completely rule her husbands by exhausting them sexually. Prior to the weddings with old men, she has already secured control of the joint property, so once she rules the bed, all mastery is hers. Any woe is then the husband's while she remains free to do as she pleases, even if what she pleases involves infidelity.

In her arguments in favor of matrimony as opposed to celibacy, the Wife of Bath is particularly virulent in her opposition to the anti-feminism she seems to have frequently encountered with the medieval clergy. If she is to be believed, her fifth husband was a former cleric who read aloud to her from anti-feminist books written by what she feels were impotent old priests who knew nothing of life or of women. She finds their attitudes infuriating.

Ironically, this strong character does not see that she is exactly the type of woman the clerics preached against. Furthermore, she seems oblivious to the way matters have changed in her own marriages as she has grown older. Because she is now less attractive and less energetic, now an older woman, her younger husbands placed her in the position her first husbands were with her. The fourth husband and Jenkin start marriage in the ascendancy; however, the formidable Wife of Bath ultimately gains the upper hand in these relationships as well.

The story told by the Wife is somewhere between a folktale and a romance. The fairies, elves, and the old hag with magic power characterize folktales, while the Arthurian court, the noble central characters, and the old woman's sermon on the true nature of gentility are characteristic of the romance. Chaucer's sources appear, in this instance, to have been solely English, derived from old tales of Sir Gawaine and from Gower's tale of Florent. Again, though, Chaucer's particular genius is evident in the combining and altering of elements from all three sources to make a tale entirely new.

Because the story is about an old woman who desires a younger man and ultimately proves wise enough to win his love and sexual attentions, it is entirely fitting that the Wife of Bath should be the narrator. The theme is obvious: the man must give the woman the upper hand in marriage if he wishes to be happy.

Study Questions

1. At what age was the Wife of Bath first married?
2. Name two arguments that the Wife uses in her defense of the married state.
3. What is the Wife's "philosophy" of marriage?
4. How has the Wife changed as she has aged?
5. In what way were her fourth and fifth husbands different from the first three?
6. What ongoing argument begins in this prologue?
7. What type of tale does the Wife tell?
8. For what crime is the young knight being punished?

9. Why is it fitting that this tale should be told by the Wife of Bath?

10. How does the ending of the story reconcile with the Wife's philosophy?

Answers

1. The Wife of Bath was 12 when she first married.

2. Her arguments for marriage include: God would not have given humans sexual organs if He did not intend for them to be used, and many people have too much sexual energy for the celibate state.

3. The wife must control the marriage in all areas.

4. She is less attractive and less energetic.

5. The first three were old and easy to control; the last two were young and tried to control her.

6. The feud between the Friar and the Summoner.

7. A cross between a folktale and a romance.

8. He has ravished (raped) a young maiden.

9. It concerns a young man marrying an old woman.

10. In the end, the young man gives in entirely to his wife and realizes the advantages of marrying an older woman.

Suggested Essay Topics

1. What clerical attitudes about women are attacked by the Wife of Bath?

2. What is ironic about her anger against these attitudes?

The Friar's Tale

Summary

The Friar says it is time to speak of "gayer things" and volunteers to tell a tale he knows about a summoner. He adds that

everyone knows how hated summoners are. The Host is afraid the Friar will upset the pilgrim Summoner, but the pilgrim Summoner says that he will shortly pay the Friar back. The Friar begins.

An archdeacon kept in his employ a summoner who had no rival for finding sinners. The man kept a network of spies to help him discover wrongdoers. He often pretended that he had charges against an individual, but if that person would compensate him, the charges would be "dismissed." By extorting money in this manner, the summoner grew rich; he shared only a little of what he collected with the archdeacon.

One day, as the rogue was on his way to charge an old widow, he meets a vigorous yeoman on the road to whom he takes an instant liking. This yeoman is a bailiff, the summoner's civil counterpart. When their conversation reveals their mutual dishonesty, lack of conscience, and love of gold, the summoner and the bailiff pledge eternal brotherhood.

Later in the trip, the summoner asks the bailiff's name and learns that he is a fiend, a devil who can alter his shape at will. He explains that he sometimes does the devil's work and sometimes inflicts God's punishments. The yeoman/demon gives the summoner a chance to forsake him, but the summoner renews his oath to be a faithful brother.

The two hear a carter stuck in the mud curse his animals to hell. The summoner wonders why the fiend does not immediately take the man up on his curse, but he soon learns that not all prayers to the devil are sincere.

When the two approach the old widow and the summoner attempts to extort money from her, she curses him sincerely. The fiend immediately grabs the summoner and takes him to hell. The Friar ends his tale promising a similar fate to all summoners.

Analysis

The Friar insults the Summoner, continuing the feud the two began earlier. He then uses his tale to intensify the insult. In his tale are all the elements of the fabliau: the plot unfolds scene by scene; it turns on trickery; and the ease with which a stupid man is outsmarted. The Friar's Tale also has elements of the exemplum, a perfect story of terrible behavior with a moral ending.

This story of the summoner meeting the devil is found in earlier Latin and German versions and had also been told in English. This problem with an exploitive clergy was an ancient one, and it is somewhat ironic that while the story is intended to condemn the Summoner, it actually condemns all extortioners, many of whom were friars. Nevertheless, the theme is unmistakable: the relationship between avarice and the devil is extremely close and will land its practitioners in hell very quickly.

Study Questions

1. What insulting remark about summoners is made by the Friar in his prologue?

2. How does the pilgrim Summoner respond to the insult?

3. In what way might a sinner in the tale have the charges of the summoner dismissed?

4. Who does the stranger he meets say he is?

5. What causes the summoner in the tale to declare eternal brotherhood for the stranger?

6. What is the real identity of the stranger?

7. Why don't the farmer's curses send his animal to hell?

8. Why do the curses of the old woman have the result of sending the summoner to hell?

9. What is the theme of this story?

10. What genres are combined in the tale?

Answers

1. He says everyone knows that no good can be said of any summoner.

2. He says he will pay the Friar back when he tells his own tale.

3. He could give the summoner money.

4. He says he is a bailiff.

5. The similarities in their work and philosophies cause the summoner and the bailiff to declare eternal brotherhood:

they are both greedy and victimize anyone with even the smallest amount of money.

6. He is a demon from hell.

7. The farmer's curses are not sincere; they just reflect his momentary anger.

8. The old woman's curses are totally sincere.

9. The relationship between avarice and its disciples is very close; it will land the avaricious man in hell very quickly.

10. It has qualities of the fabliau and of the exemplum.

Suggested Essay Topics

1. In what ways can this tale be considered an example of a fabliau? What feature of the exemplum does it contain?

2. Why is it ironic that the Friar accuse the Summoner of avarice?

The Summoner's Tale

Summary

The pilgrim Summoner is so enraged at the condemnation of the Friar that he immediately tells an evil little joke about an angel touring a friar around hell. When the visiting friar comments that he sees no friars in hell, the angel takes him directly to Satan who reveals 20,000 friars hiding in his ass, the idea being that Satan and friars are extremely close. He then tells his tale.

There was once a very greedy friar who was licensed to beg and preach in a particular district. He would pretend to have his scribe record all the names of those who donated so that his monastery could pray for them, but the names were erased as soon as he was out of sight.

On the day this story takes place, the friar calls on one of his most generous benefactors whom he finds full of anger and very ill. The friar pretends concern and swears that he and all his brother friars have been praying for Thomas to recover. He delivers a

hypocritical sermon on the great virtue in fasting, interpreting the scriptures to suit his purposes, in order to persuade Thomas to make another large donation.

The furious Thomas remarks that he cannot understand why his health has not improved with all the money he has donated for prayers (which he seems to suspect have never been offered). In reply, the friar delivers a second sermon on the terrible fate which befell famous kings who were wrathful and angry. The friar concludes by urging Thomas to give generously to the dear, poor monks who have prayed for him.

Thomas appears to agree. He says he will give the monastery something very special which he has hidden in his rectum. He instructs the friar to reach under his buttocks to retrieve the treasure. When the greedy, avaricious friar complies, Thomas expels gas loudly into the friar's hand and tells him to take that benefice and divide it with his fellow monks.

The infuriated Friar John rushes to the lord of the village for retribution. But the nobleman is so fascinated with the problem of how the fart could possibly be divided into even parts that he totally ignores the problem of retribution.

The tale is concluded with the squire's serving boy offering a solution to the division problem for the price of a new suit. The insult is never addressed, Thomas goes unpunished, and the pageboy gets a new suit.

Analysis

In his prologue, the Summoner comments immediately on the close relationship between avarice and the devil by telling a wicked joke. His tale, which follows, continues the insult in the form of a fabliau. It turns on trickery, deception, and the ease with which the evil man, in this case the friar of the story, is outwitted. Unlike the other fabliaux in the *Tales*, however, The Summoner's Tale is truly base and obscene, revealing him to be of a prurient nature.

There appear to be no models for this story; rather, it is presented as a parody of sincere religious stories which preachers used in those days to teach their listeners moral lessons. By the end of this particular story, a friendly, professional rivalry between the Summoner and the Friar has degenerated into open quarrelling through stories in which each man has damned his opponent to hell.

Study Questions

1. What is the reaction of the Summoner to The Friar's Tale?

2. What happens in the Summoner's joke about the friars?

3. What happened to the prayers that were supposed to be offered for all who donated to the friars?

4. Why is Thomas so angry with the friar?

5. How does the friar try to calm his benefactor's anger?

6. What new donation does Thomas make by way of response to the friar's sermon?

7. To whom does the friar take his case against Thomas?

8. What distracts the lord of the shire from dealing with the insult?

9. Who finally solves the problem of dividing the "gift"?

10. What does the lord's failure to punish such an insult against the clergy say about his own attitude toward friars?

Answers

1. He is infuriated.

2. A friar visiting hell finds thousands of his fellow monks tucked in the devil's rectum, as close as they can possibly get to him.

3. All the names of those who donate are erased so the prayers never get offered.

4. Thomas doesn't understand why he has not gotten well with all the prayers he has purchased.

5. The friar preaches a sermon about what happened to men who became angry and vindictive.

6. He gives the friar a fart.

7. The friar goes to the overlord of the district.

8. He becomes distracted by the problem of dividing the fart into equal parts.

9. The young squire of the lord concocts an outlandish solution.

10. Apparently, the lord finds the monks as dishonest as Thomas did.

Suggested Essay Topics

1. Explain which genre this tale fits and why.

2. What has happened to the friendly feud between the Summoner and the Friar?

The Cleric's Tale

Summary

The jovial Host teases the young Cleric for his quiet, demure behavior, but begs him to tell them a gay story with no preaching and no rhetoric. This gentler clergyman, in contrast with the two who preceded him, mildly agrees to relate a tale first written by Francis Petrarch, an Italian poet whom the Cleric revered.

The First Part: The Marquis of Saluzzo was a handsome and admired young squire who was also a bachelor. His people persuaded him that it was time to marry and even offered to pick his bride for him. He declined the offer, preferring to select his own wife, but did set a date for the wedding and commanded that all preparations be made.

The Second Part: Walter of Saluzzo surprised everyone by choosing a peasant girl for his bride. She was beautiful and virtuous. Walter had noticed her many times as he rode through his domain. The maiden was named Griselda. She was the daughter of Janicula, the poorest of all the Marquis' farmers.

With utmost courtesy, Walter asks Janicula for the hand of his daughter in marriage. Janicula, totally awestruck, assents. The Marquis then speaks to Griselda herself, conditioning their union on her agreement to obey him implicitly and never to grumble about his decisions. The virtuous Griselda agrees to obey Walter in all things and the two are wed.

The couple appears to be very happy together despite the difference in their stations in life. Griselda soon bears a lovely baby daughter.

The Third Part: Although Griselda has been unfailingly dutiful and loving, the Marquis decides that he must test her loyalty. He secretly arranges for his gruff sergeant to take the little baby girl from Griselda, telling the mother that the Marquis commanded him and behaving as if he intends to kill the child. The sergeant is then to transport the child to the sister of the Marquis in another kingdom where the infant will be lovingly reared.

Led to believe that only in this way can her husband retain the loyalty of his people, Griselda makes no protest as her child is removed. Although her heart is broken, Griselda reveals her pain in no way. True to her agreement, she completely complies with her husband's decision and he is greatly pleased.

The Fourth Part: Seven years after the birth of their daughter, the couple has a baby boy. Again, the Marquis begins to wonder about the loyalty of his wife. He tests her again in the same manner, requiring her to give up this second child. Again, Griselda is perfectly obedient and does not betray her grief in the slightest way.

The people begin to speak ill of Walter in earnest, but he persists in doubting his wife. When their daughter is 12, Walter persuades the Pope at Rome to issue a false bull (an edict from the Pope) permitting Walter to put Griselda aside and take a wife more pleasing to his subjects.

The Marquis then secretly orders his brother-in-law to return the children to Saluzzo, revealing their parentage to no one. People were to be told that the young daughter was going to be married to the Marquis of Saluzzo.

The Fifth Part: The cruel Marquis then puts Griselda to her next test. He casts her off, back to her impoverished father, wearing nothing but her shift. Without a word of protest, Griselda goes, again not revealing her terrible pain.

The Sixth Part: As the false bridal procession approaches Saluzzo, Walter applies the final test. He sends for Griselda and orders her to prepare the sleeping rooms for his new bride and her escort. This Griselda does quietly, working harder than anyone else.

When the beautiful 12-year-old girl and her entourage arrive, all the people of Saluzzo are dazzled. They begin to change their attitude and to approve the Marquis' decision to remarry. Their fickleness in contrast to Griselda's faithfulness disgusts Walter and he determines to praise Griselda at long last.

Meanwhile, Griselda helps the wedding party to be comfortable in her former home. When the Marquis asks her about her opinion of his new bride, Griselda compliments her generously. At this, the Marquis takes Griselda in his arms and kisses her, commending her greatly for her faithfulness to him and swearing his own undying love for her. He presents their children to Griselda who swoons with joy and amazement. The story ends happily with the reunited family living in harmony and love all the rest of their days.

The Cleric concludes by assuring the company that he certainly does not encourage this extreme testing of wives by their husbands. He does intend, however, that all people behave as well as Griselda did when God tests their faith with adversity.

Chaucer's Envoy: This unidentified speaker hastens to encourage women to speak up; never to allow themselves to be mistreated as Griselda was. He strongly encourages women to be men's equals and to insist on being treated well.

The Host says that he wishes his own bullying wife could have heard this story. He adds that he knows that his wife will never be meek and gentle.

Analysis

As might be expected of a scholar, the Cleric uses his prologue to express his devotion to Petrarch, most famous of the medieval Italian poets and one with whom Chaucer was very familiar. The Cleric is speaking for Chaucer in his enthusiastic admiration. Many elements of the story of Griselda come from Petrach and much of it is modelled from a tale in Boccaccio's *Decameron*.

Chaucer's version of this Italian story, however, combines elements of the romance (joyful ending, noble characters) with the promise, the magic, and the testing which characterize a folktale. However, the tale is probably intended to be considered an exemplum with its strong moral lesson and its perfect character, Griselda. The hearer is to marvel at Griselda's faithfulness but is never expected to imitate it; rather, he is at all costs to avoid behaving as Walter did in applying cruel and irrational tests to the loyalty of those he loves.

Study Questions

1. What promise does Griselda make to Walter before accepting his offer of marriage?

2. Name each of the tests Walter applies to test Griselda's loyalty.

3. Does Walter ever relent in his testing of his wife?

4. On which two Italian classics is The Cleric's Tale based?

5. Which two genres are represented in this story?

6. Why does Walter not allow the people to select his wife for him?

7. How does Walter use public opinion to persuade the Pope to grant nullification of his marriage?

8. When she comes to her father's house, who do the people think Walter's daughter is?

9. How is the hearer intended to respond to this tale?

10. What does "Chaucer's Envoy" add?

Answers

1. She will be an absolutely obedient wife and never question his decisions or complain about them.

2. First, he takes away their firstborn daughter. Then, he takes away their son. Finally, he casts her off as his wife, forcing her to prepare the house for his new bride.

3. At the end of the story, when he has taken everything from her, he relents and they live happily after.

4. This tale is based on the writings of Petrarch, and Boccaccio's *Decameron*.

5. It combines the elements of the romance and the exemplum.

6. He thinks his peasants are not wise enough to choose his bride.

7. He persuades the Pope that his people are turning against Griselda since she is lowborn.

8. They have heard that she is to be his new wife.

9. The hearer is intended to avoid behaving as Walter did while still admiring Griselda.

10. The "Envoy" advises women never to take such abuse from their husbands, but to speak up when they are treated unfairly.

Suggested Essay Topics

1. Although she is exaggerated, Griselda is a model of the medieval clerical idea of woman. Based on the character, explain the clergy's ideal of the model wife.

2. Contrast Griselda with the Wife of Bath.

The Merchant's Tale

Summary

Commenting that his wife is absolutely nothing like Griselda, the Merchant reveals that he is very unhappily married. The Host, who can sympathize, begs the Merchant to tell more. Saying he would prefer not to go on about his own troubles, the Merchant begins his story.

January is an Italian knight who has remained a bachelor for 60 years. However, he has recently become convinced that the married state is the happiest and has, therefore, decided that he will take a wife.

January calls in all of his friends and brothers and lectures them all on the bliss of the wedded state. He then begs them to help him find a young wife because he wants to marry right away. Some advise him against haste and others against marrying a young woman, but January's mind is made up on both scores.

Over the next several days, January imagines all the town's eligible women and considers their virtues and attractiveness. His choice finally rests on May, a girl of 20 who is poor, but very beautiful. He is overjoyed with his decision, but troubled because he has heard that man may be allowed true bliss only once. January is

afraid that the joy he anticipates in marriage will prevent his enjoying eternal bliss in heaven.

The eager bridegroom's brother reminds him of the commentary of the Wife of Bath (it is unknown how she came to be in this story) and assures him that it is unlikely that he has anything about which to be concerned.

January soon marries May and commences his life of marital bliss. However, all is not well because, the Merchant tells us, January's handsome young squire, Damian, is so in love with May that he is nearly overcome with passion. He writes a love poem to the bride, puts it in a silken purse, and wears it next to his heart until the opportunity presents itself to give it to May.

Within a few days of the wedding, Damian takes to his bed. When May and her ladies visit him, Damian slips the love letter to May who hides it on her person. After reading and destroying the poem, May decides that she is in love with the handsome Damian. She declares her fondness and willingness in a secret letter which she gives him a few days later.

Meanwhile, January is foolishly happy. He has a secret garden to which only he has the key. There he and May frolic and frequently make love. One day, however, January is suddenly struck blind. From that point on, he becomes so fearful of losing May that he insists she remain close enough for him to touch at all times. After a short period of adjustment, January and May resume their lovemaking in the garden.

During the early days of her husband's blindness, May has secretly had a copy of the only garden key made and has given it to Damian. One day, Damian enters the secret garden before May and January arrive. When the couple enters the garden, May pretends to want a pear. Assuming them to be totally alone in the garden, January permits his wife to climb the tree to pick some fruit. Damian is already in the tree so he and May immediately begin frantic lovemaking there.

At that same moment, the King and Queen of Fairyland are debating about the situation going on under January's nose. The King resolves to restore January's sight so that he may witness and avenge the adultery. His Queen, however, assures him that she will give May the words to totally exonerate herself and dupe January even further.

Instantly, January's sight is restored. He looks up to find Damian and May madly making love in the tree. Enraged, he screams that he has been betrayed. May glibly tells him that the only way for his sight to be restored was for her to struggle with a man in a tree. When January says he knows what he saw, and what he saw was not a struggle but a passionate sexual joining, May contradicts him. She convinces January, who wants to believe her, that his state of blindness had made his newly restored vision a little out of focus at first.

May climbs down from the tree. January leads her back to the palace where they live happily ever after. What happens to Damian is not confided. The tale ends.

The Host comments that women are naturally deceptive. He adds that although his wife is faithful, she has many, many other faults which he will not list because someone in the group would be sure to tell his wife. That is how women are, the Host confides; they stick together.

Analysis

This tale is another example of fabliau with its deceiving, tricking, and making a fool of a foolish man. The elements of the romance (i.e., the knight, the rituals, the gardens, the palace) are inserted to add humor and contrast to the tale of an earthy young woman who determines to enjoy her young lover and gets away with it.

As with many of the tales, the material for this story is drawn from many sources: Italian, German, and French literature, as well as English oral tradition.

The theme of blindness dominates this tale. January is too blind to see his foolishness in marrying such a young woman. After the marriage, his love and his desire to be happy blind him to May's infidelity. His physical blindness reinforces the theme.

The Merchant's Tale is also about marriage. It reiterates the message in earlier tales: men are always taken in and manipulated by their wives, suffering greatly in the process. Not only is this true for January, but for the Merchant and the Host as well.

Study Questions

1. Describe the trickery and deception used to dupe January.
2. What is the literary genre of The Merchant's Tale?
3. What elements of the romance are incorporated?
4. What is the theme of this tale?
5. What is this story saying about marriage?
6. What does the Merchant reveal about his own marriage in his prologue?
7. Who sympathizes with him?
8. What is the significance of the names of the husband and wife in this tale?
9. What is the function of the advisors to the old knight?
10. Why is it appropriate that this tale be told by the Merchant?

Answers

1. Instances of trickery include Damian and May secretly passing notes; May making a key to the secret garden; May claiming she is following the orders of the gods; and May convincing January that he did not really see what he thought he saw when she and her lover are caught.
2. It is a fabliau.
3. The knight, the rituals, the gardens, and the palace are all elements of the romance.
4. Men are easily manipulated and made fools of by their wives.
5. Old men should not marry extremely young women.
6. He is very unhappily married.
7. The Host sympathizes with him.
8. January represents winter, the last of the cycles of life while May symbolizes spring when everything is new and lovely. These names refer to the ages of the characters.

9. They serve to demonstrate that January will not listen to any advice in this matter but is determined to do things his own way.

10. The Merchant is older and has possibly been the victim of a younger, unfaithful wife.

Suggested Essay Topics

1. How does The Merchant's Tale resemble the fabliaux that precede it?

2. Why would the Wife of Bath approve of May's behavior?

The Squire's Tale (Fragment)

Summary

The Host invites the Squire to tell a love story, assuming the youth to be knowledgeable in such matters. The Squire says he really does not know that much, but he agrees to tell a story.

The First Part: In the land of the Tatars there lived a noble and famous king called Cambiuskan, who possessed every conceivable virtue and knightly trait. Cambiuskan and his queen had two sons and a gorgeous young daughter, Canace.

The story begins in the twentieth year of Cambiuskan's reign. In the early spring, he announces his birthday feast, as was his custom. As the glorious feast begins, the guests are suddenly amazed to see a knight on a brass horse, wearing a bare sword, ride into the hall. On his thumb is a marvelous gold ring, and he is holding a large glass mirror in his hand.

Eloquently, the mysterious knight addresses Cambiuskan, saying that he brings the gifts on behalf of his liege lord, the King of Arabia and India. He then explains the marvelous gifts. The wondrous horse will ride or even fly the king anywhere he wants to go. It can even make itself invisible. The sword will cut through armor; no man it wounds will ever be healed unless the king lays the flat of the magical sword upon the wound he has inflicted.

The ring is for Canace. It will enable her to understand the language of birds and to decipher the uses of all healing herbs. She

will have these powers whenever she wears the ring on her person. The mirror will allow her to see clearly any treachery in the heart of a man who courts her.

The Second Part: Everyone at the feast marvels at the gifts except Canace, who retires early. Next morning she rises at dawn and dresses to walk in the lovely spring morning. Wearing the magical ring, she could understand the songs of the birds.

As Canace strolls along, she hears the pitiful wailing of a female falcon who is bleeding from her self-inflicted wounds. The tender-hearted Canace understands that the bird is suffering terribly and has the bird tell her story.

It turns out that the lovely lady falcon has fallen in love with a noble male who has falsely pledged his undying love for her. They lived together joyfully for a time, but now her mate has deserted her and has fallen madly in love with a kite. The kite has held the male falcon's love, and the female is absolutely desolate without him. Grief and anger at her plight have caused her to tear her own flesh.

Canace takes the falcon to her quarters, bandages her wounds, and builds her a lovely cage which she keeps above the head of her bed. The female falcon begins to heal, but she continues her grieving.

The Squire here leaves Canace and promises to tell about Cambiuskan with his magic horse and enchanted sword.

The Third Part: One sentence fragment…and the Squire's story stops. Chaucer never completed it.

The Franklin greatly admires the Squire's obvious education and his eloquence in storytelling. He says he wishes that he could persuade his own son to take his education more seriously and leave off gambling. He also wishes the boy were as courteous as the young squire. The Host intrudes to demand that the Franklin tell his tale.

Analysis

The prologue to the tale refers back to the deceitful nature of women and looks ahead to a tale of pure and ideal love.

Though it is incomplete, The Squire's Tale is obviously going to be a romance. All indications are that it would have been an intricate one with several plot threads and several important characters.

The interesting device of setting a story within a story is used with the falcon's tale of an unfaithful lover. This insertion is probably meant either to foreshadow or to contrast with the love story planned for Canace.

Like others of the tales Chaucer invented, this one has roots in both French and English literature, but unlike any other of Chaucer's stories, The Squire's Tale reveals considerable Oriental influence. This adds an exotic quality absent in the other tales.

There is little mystery, however, as regards the theme of this narration. It strongly promises to deal with wonders, constancy in love, and virtuous character. Ideal love will no doubt triumph in the end.

Study Questions

1. What element is inserted in The Squire's Tale that is not present in any of the others?

2. What is the probable theme of this tale?

3. What elements of the romance are present in this fragment?

4. What type of tale is the falcon's story intended to imitate?

5. What gifts does the mysterious knight bring Cambiuskan?

6. Describe the magical properties of each of the gifts.

7. Who has sent the strange knight?

8. What event is being celebrated when the bearer of gifts enters?

9. Why does the Host invite the Squire to tell a love story?

10. What is the Franklin's opinion of the Squire?

Answers

1. This tale has Oriental or exotic qualities.

2. Ideal love prevails.

3. Noble characters, ideal womanhood, and elements of magic and the supernatural are romantic elements of this fragment.

4. The falcon's story imitates a beast fable.

5. The mysterious knight brings Cambiuskan a brass horse, a sword, a ring, and a mirror.

6. The horse can take the King anywhere and it can fly. The ring enables its wearer to understand the language of birds. The sword can cut through armor and wounds inflicted with this sword can be healed only with the touch of this sword. The mirror enables Canace to know the heart of any man who courts her.

7. The King of Arabia and India has sent the knight.

8. Cambiuskan's birthday is the celebrated event.

9. In the General Prologue, the Squire is described as a young lover. As such, he should be able to tell an apt love story.

10. The Franklin admires the Squire's learning and language greatly.

Suggested Essay Topics

1. In what ways does Canace meet the standards for ideal womanhood?

2. Explain the exotic qualities of this story.

The Franklin's Tale

Summary

The Franklin tells the company that the ancient Bretons made up rhymed stories which they set to music. He says he is uneducated but can tell one of the traditional Breton tales.

In Brittany, a noble knight falls in love with an honorable lady. When she learns of his love, the lady agrees to take the knight as her husband. The knight is overjoyed. In his enthusiasm, he volunteers never to be jealous or to try to rule her. His wife need only let it appear as though he is the master in the marriage.

Arveragus and Dorigen marry; but after about a year, Arveragus announces that he must go to London for a year or two in order to

win knightly honor and glory in arms. As soon as her husband leaves, Dorigen becomes ill with longing for Arveragus. She weeps both night and day and refuses all comfort.

Finally, her friends persuade her that her mood can be improved by walking along the seashore near her palace. On her walks, Dorigen would sometimes rest on a cliff above the shore and look down at the huge, horrible black rocks below. At these moments of solitude, she is filled with an irrational fear. She hates the rocks and sees no reason for their ever having been created.

One day, while enjoying a spring festival, Dorigen encounters Aurelius, a handsome, lust squire who has loved her secretly for a long time. Because he is her neighbor and a respectable man, Dorigen engages Aurelius in conversation. Encouraged by her interest in him, the squire grows bold and declares his love for Dorigen, which he knows to be in vain.

Dorigen responds to his declaration of love by saying that she can never be an unfaithful wife. Then, jokingly, she adds that she will become his love on the day when he removes all the terrible black rocks from the coast of Britanny.

Aurelius goes home and begins to plead with the gods for a miracle which will remove all the rocks. Aurelius then falls unconscious, having become ill from his unrequited love. His brother carries him to bed.

After the two years have passed, Arveragus comes home. He and Dorigen resume their marital happiness.

For the two years following his encounter with Dorigen, Aurelius has lain in a terrible sickness, nursed by his faithful brother who is filled with concern. When Aurelius regains enough strength to move about, the cleric brother sees that Aurelius is still vulnerable as the lovesickness is still in his heart.

The brother remembers a book of magic that he had heard of when he was at university. He resolves to find a colleague from Orleans familiar with the magic so that his brother can be cured.

Aurelius and his brother go off to Orleans where the first person they meet is a young cleric who is also a magician. They go home with him to a place where there is unbelievable abundance spread before them. The mysterious cleric shows them marvelous visions, including one in which Aurelius is dancing with Dorigen. The brothers understand that they are in the presence of a powerful magician.

Aurelius and his brother haggle with the magician over his fee for removing the rocks from Britanny's coast. After they agree upon a great price, Aurelius's heart is at last calm.

The next day the magician returns with the brothers to their home and begins to work immediately to create his illusion. After six months of computing and figuring, in the month of December, the magician is able to make the rocks seem to disappear.

Aurelius rushes to the temple of Venus where he finds Dorigen and tells her of this miracle. He implores her to keep her word and love him best or he will die. Terribly upset, Dorigen goes home full of sorrow feeling that she must now choose between death and dishonor. To her, death is preferable. She contemplates suicide.

A few days later, Arveragus returns from a short trip and finds his wife in terrible sadness. When she confides to him the problem he says, in his great generosity to her and to Aurelius, that she must keep her promise.

As Dorigen is on her way to a garden to keep her promise to Aurelius, she encounters the young knight in the busiest part of the town. She reveals her destination and tells Aurelius that Arveragus has ordered her to keep her promise. Amazed at the husband's generosity and deeply compassionate at Dorigen's obvious reluctance, Aurelius decides he would rather have his passion remain unsatisfied than have Dorigen suffer from his insistence. He releases her from her promise, citing Arveragus for his unbelievable generosity.

Aurelius returns to his home where he tells the magician that he can only pay him half of the gold that he had pledged now, but that he will pay the other half no matter if he has to sell everything he has to do so. When the magician inquires as to the outcome of the affair with Dorigen, Aurelius tells him everything. The magician responds that he can do no less than Arveragus and Aurelius have done. He forgives Aurelius all of the debt and rides away.

The Franklin ends his story by asking the listeners to judge which of the three men was the most generous.

Analysis

At the end of The Squire's Tale, the Franklin effusively praises the Squire's scholarship and affected language. He is revealed to be an imitator of the nobility so it is no wonder that he introduces his tale by apologizing for not having had the education of a noble. His lack of training requires him to speak in plain language. Actually, the Franklin displays extensive learning in this introduction, citing numerous classical references and attempting a clumsy rhetorical pun.

The Franklin tells a tale which he hopes might have been told by a noble, as romances were supposed to be confined in circulation to the nobility. His romance centers on ideal love, the virtuous woman, and the capacity of Man to be supremely generous and to behave according to the knightly ideal. Further confirming his tale as a romance, the Franklin includes noble characters, a classical setting, and elements of magic which give a hint of the mysterious and otherworldly. The rash promise made without reflection and possibly, without intent to fulfill, are further features of the romance.

Just as the Franklin relates, one of Chaucer's sources for this story is the Breton lais. He has also borrowed from the writings of St. Jerome; from Boccaccio's *Decameron*; and from the French *Le Roman de la Rose*.

Like most of the tales, The Franklin's Tale concentrates on the relationship between husbands, wives, and lovers, exposing the vices and virtues of men and women. All of the characters in this particular story are virtuous, unlike those presented in the fabliaux. There is nothing crass about Aurelius and Dorigen, for although both of them err, all are shown in the end to be capable of great honor, loyalty, and generosity. The sanctity of marriage is upheld and respected in The Franklin's Tale.

Study Questions

1. What quality of the nobility does the Franklin admire most and try to imitate in his tale?

2. What is the rash promise made by Dorigen which is the source of all the trouble in The Franklin's Tale?

3. In what literary genre is this story written?

4. What is the theme of this tale?

5. From what sources did Chaucer borrow in creating The Franklin's Tale?

6. What is the effect on Aurelius when Dorigen rebuffs him?

7. Who stands by Aurelius during all of his trials?

8. How is the impossible feat of removing the rocks finally accomplished?

9. When he cannot pay his debt, what does Aurelius promise to do?

10. What does the magician do in response?

Answers

1. Education is what the Franklin admires and imitates.

2. She promises to love Aurelius if he can remove the frightening stones.

3. Romance is this tale's genre.

4. The nature of marriage and the faithfulness of the good wife are two of its themes.

5. The story is based on a Breton lais; but Chaucer has also borrowed from the writings of St. Jerome; Boccaccio's *Decameron*; and *Le Roman de la Rose*.

6. He falls desperately ill for two years.

7. His brother takes care of Aurelius.

8. The brothers hire a magician who performs the illusion.

9. He says he will pay the balance even if he has to sell everything he owns.

10. He cancels Aurelius' debt.

Suggested Essay Topics

1. How does Dorigen fit into the medieval concept of woman-hood?

2. Why would the Franklin, a member of the middle class, tell this story of the nobility?

The Physician's Tale

Summary

This is the only story which is not linked to the others by dialogue among the pilgrims.

Virginius, a noble knight of Old Rome, had the loveliest daughter anyone could imagine. She was Nature's perfect work; and Virginia's virtue was a thousand times greater than her beauty. She was particularly prudent with regard to preserving her chastity. To protect her purity, Virginia often pretended to be ill so that she wouldn't be vulnerable to the wantonness prevalent at dances, feasts, and revels.

One day, when Virginia goes to pray at the temple, a very famous judge called Appius observes the maiden and immediately determines to ravish her. Conspiring with a fellow called Claudius, Appius persuades the man to testify falsely that Virginia is really a slave girl, born into Claudius' house and stolen from him in the night when she was very young. Virginius is summoned to the court to hear the charges but is given no chance to testify or to call witnesses. The lascivious Appius rules that Virginia is to be immediately returned to Claudius, her rightful owner.

The heartbroken Virginius goes to his home immediately and lays the situation before his beloved daughter. Both are aware of Appius' evil intentions and Virginius tells his daughter that he must kill her rather than allow her to be dishonored in this way. She asks if there is any other way to save her. Her father replies in the negative.

Requesting a little time to grieve, Virginia faints with shock and sorrow. When she recovers, Virginia declares her thanks to God that she is permitted to die a virgin. Begging her father to sever her head gently, Virginia again falls into a swoon. Virginius cuts off the head of his unconscious child and bears it to the judge.

The furious Appius commands that Virginius be hanged, but at that exact moment, 1,000 citizens burst into the court to save the valiant knight. Appius is then thrown into prison where he commits suicide; Claudius is exiled; and all the others involved in the conspiracy are hanged.

The Physician concludes by admonishing his listeners that their sins, no matter how jealously guarded, are known to God; and that God will punish wickedness in every man without regard to rank.

Analysis

This legend of a girl saved from dishonor when her father kills her is an echo of the preceding tale told by the Franklin. Although Dorigen was a married woman, she mentions stories like the Physician's, and she herself contemplates suicide rather than succumb to sexual dishonor. The characters in both these stories are pagans. The similarities between the two stories is deliberate on Chaucer's part; it is one of the devices he uses to unify the whole of *The Canterbury Tales.*

While this story of the pitiable Virginia is intended as an exemplum containing as it does a model of virtue for the listener to imitate, Virginia's chastity does not benefit her. She dies because of it and no eternal reward is mentioned. In the story that precedes this one, however, Dorigen's virtue is rewarded with release from her odious promise. St. Cecelia, in the tale which follows, dies a virgin also, but her reward is eternal life.

Chaucer took the story of Virginius and his daughter from *Le Roman de la Rose,* making a noticeable change only in the killing of Virginia. In the original, Virginius beheads the maiden in public, while Chaucer makes the killing a private matter.

That virtuous women prefer death to sexual dishonor is the obvious theme of this tale. It may also be observed that the horrible outcome points to the horror which results when justice is corrupted. Virginius represents true justice while Appius personifies justice corrupted.

Study Questions

1. What characteristic of an exemplum is found in The Physician's Tale?

2. How are The Franklin's Tale, The Physician's Tale, and The Second Nun's Tale alike?

3. In what way are they different?

4. What is the theme of The Physician's Tale?

5. In what way does Virginius represent true justice and how does Appius represent justice corrupted?

6. How does Virginia, though pagan, fit into the medieval Christian concept of virtuous womanhood?

7. How did Chaucer change his tale from the original?

8. On what source is The Physician's Tale based?

9. What trumped up charges put Virginia under the control of the evil judge?

10. How is Virginius saved from Appius' outrage when Virginius defies the wicked order to turn his daughter over to the court?

Answers

1. It contains a model of virtue in Virginia; she is perfectly pure and perfectly obedient.

2. All of them contain examples of virtuous women.

3. Virginia receives no reward for her purity; Dorigen receives an earthly reward; and St. Cecelia is granted an eternal reward for her chastity.

4. A virtuous woman will prefer death to dishonor.

5. Virginius has motives which are completely pure and honorable, while Appius is motivated by his lustful desire.

6. She accepts death rather than sexual soiling.

7. In the original tale, Virginius kills his daughter in public. In Chaucer's tale, it is a private act.

8. It is based on the French work *Le Roman de la Rose.*

9. She is accused of being a runaway slave girl belonging to the judge's co-conspirator.

10. A large group of citizens rushes into the court to save Virginius and punish Appius.

Suggested Essay Topics

1. In what ways do Virginius and Virginia fulfill the romantic ideal?

2. What elements of the Republic of Rome are present in this tale?

The Pardoner's Tale

Summary

The Host finds the Physician's story terribly touching. Teasing the Physician, he begs the Pardoner to cure the pain caused by the Physician's narrative by telling a gay story immediately. The Pardoner, denied a drink before launching his tale, punishes the company by making them wait while he thinks of a suitably moral story.

That greed is the root of all evil, the Pardoner tells the travelers, is always his theme when he preaches. He boasts openly of his corrupt practices and manipulative methods of getting money out of the gullible. He brags boldly of how little he cares for humanity. He also states that he enjoys the creature comforts humanity's guilt and stupidity afford him. The terrible man is also aware that he preaches against what he himself practices. He launches his story by remarking that his wickedness does not prevent him from telling a moral story.

Early one day, three very debauched and evil companions are drinking together in a tavern. These young men have been totally ruined by the sins of gluttony, avarice, and sloth, against which sins the narrator interjects a short sermon.

The three hear a bell tolling a funeral and a boy tells them that a friend of theirs, killed by a thief called Death, is about to be

buried. The tavern keeper says this fellow, Death, has slain a whole village about a mile from there.

The three drunks swear an oath to find Death and slay him before nightfall. They head out for the town the tavern keeper mentioned. Shortly, they meet a very old man who points them to an oak tree where he says they will meet Death.

Off rushes the besotted trio, but when they reach the oak tree, it is bushels of gold they find there. All thoughts of Death leave them as they plot to get the money back to their own village. The young men draw straws to see which of them will go back to the town for food and drink to sustain them during the day while they guard their treasure.

The youngest of the three draws the short straw; he sets out for the town at once. As soon as he is gone, the other two conspire to murder him when he returns so that they can keep the wealth all for themselves.

In the meantime, the youngest one has determined to kill the other two. He buys strong poison in the town and adds it to the wine he buys for his companions. However, as soon as the youngest gets back with the supplies, the two companions pounce on him and murder him. They then sit down to drink and make merry, but die immediately when they drink the poisoned wine.

This story is followed by another sermon against avarice and the beginning of a sales pitch for the relics the Pardoner carries, but here the Host interrupts. He refuses to go along with any more of what he perceives as the Pardoner's duplicity and sacrilege and says so very coarsely. The Pardoner becomes infuriated at the Host's insults and the Knight has to intervene. He insists that the two kiss and make up, which they do.

Analysis

The wicked practices of the Pardoner were, unfortunately, widespread in the medieval Catholic Church. However, the Pardoner is so openly and gleefully and unashamedly wicked that he himself serves a sermon against these practices. His tale is totally in keeping with his character.

The form of The Pardoner's Tale, an allegory, is one with which medieval audiences would have been completely familiar. In an allegory, the characters personify abstract qualities; the plot is meant to teach a moral lesson. In this case, Avarice, Gluttony, and Sloth meet Death at their own hands; in other words, these vices lead invariably to spiritual death.

This particular allegory had many versions in Eastern and in Western literature and was frequently enacted as a morality play. Therefore, it is not attributed to any single source. Chaucer's version is the one that has survived. It has become one of the most widely read and best loved of *The Canterbury Tales*.

Study Questions

1. What is an allegory?

2. What abstract qualities are portrayed by the evil young men in the story?

3. What is the theme of this tale?

4. What is the moral lesson of this tale?

5. What characteristics does the Pardoner reveal in his prologue?

6. How does this story fit the character of the Pardoner?

7. Why would medieval audiences have been familiar with The Pardoner's Tale?

8. How does the youngest reveler plan to kill the other two?

9. Does he kill them?

10. How does the youngest die?

Answers

1. An allegory is a tale in which the characters personify abstract qualities, usually to teach a moral lesson.

2. They represent Avarice, Gluttony, and Sloth.

3. The theme of the tale is the inevitable outcome of wickedness.

4. The moral lesson is that avarice, gluttony, and sloth lead to spiritual death.

5. He himself is totally motivated by greed and seems to have no virtue at all.

6. The young men represent all the Pardoner's own faults.

7. It was famous in both Eastern and Western literature and was often acted out as a morality play.

8. He poisons the wine that he buys for them to drink.

9. Yes; they drink the wine and die.

10. The other two young men kill the youngest as soon as he returns from town.

Suggested Essay Topics

1. Explain in detail the moral lesson conveyed in The Pardoner's Tale.

2. Give a full character description of the pilgrim Pardoner.

The Second Nun's Tale

Summary

The Nun tells the company that idleness leads to sinfulness while lawful industry is an aid to the avoidance of sin. The sister then tells the company that she will tell the life of St. Cecelia to give them an example of a good woman. She says she will tell them the version she has translated from *The Legend of Good Women.*

The tale is preceded by an Invocation to Mary in which the nun prays to be inspired to tell the story to the profit of her listeners. The Invocation is followed by a lengthy explanation of the name "Cecelia," which may be translated "lily of heaven," "the way for the blind," or "lack of blindness." If one stretches a point, it may be read "way for the people," the point being that St. Cecelia's name implies all for which she is revered.

Cecelia belonged to a noble Roman family who were Christians at a time when the Christian faith was forbidden. Nevertheless, the devout girl had promised to remain a virgin in observance of her faith. Her holiness was so sincere that an angel guarded her chastity.

On their wedding night, Cecelia persuaded her husband, Valerian, that he could see her angel if he, too, would agree to remain chaste. When Valerian agreed, Cecelia sent him to the outlawed Pope Urban who thanked God for Valerian's newfound faith. The angel of God then appeared and Valerian was instantly converted.

When Valerian returned home he found Cecelia awaiting him with the angel. The angel held crowns of lilies and roses. Giving them to the young couple, the angel promised that the crowns would never wither as long as the two remained chaste. He further assured them that the fragrant crowns would be seen only by the good and pure. As a reward for his faithfulness, Valerian was permitted one wish by the angel. Valerian requests that his brother, Tiburtius, might be converted.

When Valerian invited Tiburtius to embrace the true faith and showed him the crowns, Tiburtius, too, wanted to become a Christian. Cecelia explained to him about the mysteries of the faith and sent Tiburtius to Pope Urban to be baptized. After baptism, Tiburtius was filled with holiness and joined Cecelia and Valerian in a holy life.

The three made many converts and performed many miracles. This brought them to the attention of the Prefect who had them brought before him for interrogation. When they testified to their faith, the Prefect commanded them to make sacrifice to Jupiter on pain of death, but the Christian young people refused.

Maximus, the guard who had taken them into custody, found the young people's witness so convincing that he and his household also became Christians that same day. On the morrow, Valerian and Tiburtius were executed. When Maximus proclaimed that he could see their souls being borne to heaven by bright, shining angels, the infuriated Prefect whipped him so severely that Maximus, too, died.

Cecelia was next led to make sacrifice to Jupiter; but she, too, refused. All those around her were converted by her shining holiness. The Prefect then had Cecelia brought into his presence. Infuriated that his power and the fear of death did not intimidate the girl, the Prefect ordered a terrible death for the maiden.

Guards took her to her own home and locked her in the bath and set a roaring fire so that she would be killed by the heat. Yet after three days, Cecelia was still alive and unharmed. The Prefect then had a soldier smote her three times on the neck which left the maiden only half dead. Attended by loving Christian friends, Cecelia suffered for three more days and then died.

Upon her death, Pope Urban secretly buried Cecelia amongst other Christian martyrs. He consecrated her house the Church of Saint Cecelia, knowing her already to be in Paradise and beloved of Christ.

Analysis

There are no conversational links either before or after The Second Nun's Tale, a possible indication that this narrative is intended to be taken with complete seriousness. The tale itself is exactly what it appears to be, the life of a saint. It is taken directly from a former work by Chaucer, *The Legend of Good Women*. The listeners are getting the straight "facts" as they are related by an anonymous sister whose reverence for St. Cecelia is completely appropriate to one of her station.

In this life of St. Cecelia, Chaucer presents the contemporary Christian ideal of womanhood. Chaste, devout, strong, and intellectual, St. Cecelia is completely indomitable. Through her influence, many are converted and even more come to Christ through her death. She is womanly but not weak; indeed, she has none of the shortcomings of any of the other women characters in the tales. There is no question that she is presented to be imitated.

Study Questions

1. The Second Nun's Story is the only example of what type of story?

2. How does Cecelia maintain her virginity in marriage?

3. Why is it appropriate that this story be told by the Nun?

4. Where did the Nun learn the story of St. Cecelia?

5. Why is this slightly ironic?

6. When do angels appear in this story?

7. What may account for the absence of conversational links before and after The Second Nun's Tale?

8. For what specific refusal is Cecelia condemned to death?

9. Why doesn't the raging fire burn the young wife?

10. From what cause does St. Cecelia finally die?

Answers

1. It is an example of a saint's legend.

2. She converts her husband and obtains his promise that they will both remain virgins and never consummate the marriage.

3. She is a woman who has taken a vow of perpetual virginity; it is suitable that she should honor St. Cecelia.

4. *The Legend of Good Women* (by Geoffrey Chaucer) is her source.

5. It is ironic because Chaucer, unknown to anyone, is among the pilgrims.

6. Angels appear in this tale after Valerian has converted (angels present crowns of flowers to him and to Cecelia) and when the souls of Valerian and Tiburtius are being borne to heaven after they are martyred.

7. This story is sincerely religious and is to be taken with complete seriousness; therefore, Chaucer omitted the humorous links.

8. She will not sacrifice to Jupiter.

9. Cecelia was protected by either divine intervention or a miracle.

10. A soldier sent by Maximus smites her three times with a sword; she dies three days later from her wounds.

Suggested Essay Topics

1. Compare and contrast St. Cecelia with Virginia and Dorigen.

2. Explain how Cecelia fulfills the medieval ideal of womanhood.

The Canon's Yeoman's Tale

New Characters:

The Canon: *clergyman, generally in charge of a cathedral*

The Canon's Yeoman: *servant to the Canon*

Summary

Shortly after the tale of St. Cecelia is finished, two riders, one of whom is dressed like a canon, approach the party. They have observed the jolly group and have ridden very hard to catch up and join the party. The Host bids them welcome if the Canon is able to tell a merry tale or two. The Canon's Yeoman replies that the Canon is a very important person and certainly able to contribute to the entertainment. In fact, it is hinted that he somehow knows a very great deal about a great many things. The Host is impatient with the Yeoman's mysterious and roundabout way of speaking and tells him to come right out and say whether the man he serves is indeed a cleric. The Yeoman responds that his master is much greater than any cleric for he can turn silver into gold.

Harry Bailley does not believe the Yeoman because the two are dressed so shabbily. This comment leads the Yeoman to air his complaints against his master, the Canon, and to reveal that the man is really an alchemist. His master tries to shut him up, but the Yeoman will not stop talking. The furious Canon rides off in a huff. Then the Yeoman promises to tell all, at the same time lamenting his own involvement in this business of changing base metal into gold and bemoaning his inability to extricate himself from the business.

There once was an alchemist disguised as a canon who was terribly evil. He supported his attempts to change base metals into gold by duping innocent people out of their money.

On the occasion of this story, the alchemist talks an old and gullible priest into buying copper and quicksilver (mercury) for him and then pretends to turn them into a sheet of sterling silver. The so-called canon pretends to allow the priest to talk him into selling his magic formula for 40 pounds. The wicked alchemist then takes off with the money.

Of course, the priest has been tricked. Two times in the fake chemical processes, the quicksilver evaporated unbeknownst to the priest and the canon replaced it with liquid silver. One time, the trickster goes through the motions of turning a copper ingot (bar of metal) into silver. He actually has a silver ingot up his sleeve which he substitutes for the copper when the priest is not looking. In this way, the old clergyman, ignorant of chemistry, is convinced that the alchemist actually can turn silver into gold and is eager to buy the secret formula.

Finally, the Yeoman explains all the false efforts of his Canon and confides that they are always unsuccessful in their attempts. The only definite thing they have accomplished is the ruin of the Yeoman's complexion because his job is always to blow on the fire to make it grow hotter and hotter. The heat and noxious vapors have ruined his skin. In his heart of hearts, the Yeoman realizes that he and his master can never turn base metal to gold, yet he and his master both persist in the attempt.

Analysis

In this prologue, for the first time in the links between the tales, something besides conversation actually transpires. New characters come riding in; one stays; the other leaves. The Canon's Yeoman, who remains, reveals himself and his master to be outlaws of sorts, as well as complete shams. Yet, he is congenial and anxious to participate in the fun. He tells a biographical tale which appears to be about the Canon.

The Canon's Yeoman's Tale is not a typical medieval story. It seems to be a combination of the learning of the day about alchemy, preaching against alchemy, and biography/autobiography about the teller and his master. It is certain that alchemy was widely practiced in England at the time of *The Canterbury Tales* and that the church was strongly opposed to this pseudo-science. Ironically, alchemy was practiced almost exclusively by monks, the only ones with an adequate education in Latin to decipher the ancient texts on the subject.

It should also be noted that the narrator reveals his own complicity in the forbidden practice at the same time that he condemns it. He is a man torn. This Yeoman is so deeply involved and fascinated by alchemy that he cannot extricate himself from this secret sin. At the same time, he realizes that alchemy is probably a false and futile effort and despises himself for his persistent slavery to the slender hope that it might prove real.

Study Questions

1. In what way is the prologue to this tale different from others in *The Canterbury Tales*?

2. What is alchemy?

3. By whom was alchemy practiced and why was its practice confined to this group?

4. Why is The Canon's Yeoman's Tale different from the other tales?

5. About what does the Canon's Yeoman seem to be in conflict?

6. What angers the pilgrim Canon? What does he do because of his anger?

7. Describe the two tricks the alchemist employs to dupe the priest in the tale.

8. What is always the outcome of alchemy?

9. According to the Canon's Yeoman, what keeps people involved in the practice of alchemy?

10. What physical disfigurement have the experiments caused the Canon's Yeoman?

Answers

1. It contains action; the Canon and his Yeoman ride up to join the travelers.

2. The attempt to transmute (transform) base metals into gold.

3. Usually by the clergy; they were the only ones educated, thus the only ones who could read the ancient writings on the subject.

4. It has no known literary genre; it seems to be autobiographical/biographical.

5. He is fascinated by alchemy at the same time he recognizes its probable futility.

6. When his Yeoman begins to divulge the secret nature of their business, the Canon becomes furious and rides away.

7. One time he substitutes a gold ingot he had hidden in his sleeve for the silver; the other trick involves replacing evaporated quicksilver with liquid silver.

8. Alchemy always fails.

9. They keep hoping that the next time they will be successful.

10. His face is scarred and is a terrible color from having to blow on the fire constantly.

Suggested Essay Topics

1. Why would the medieval church forbid the practice of alchemy?

2. Discuss the kinds of dishonesty alchemy seems to require using both the Yeoman's confessions and the tale as sources.

The Manciple's Tale

Summary

The Cook had so much to drink that he has fallen asleep in the saddle. The Manciple derides and insults him for this, whereupon the Cook's drunken agitation causes him to fall off his horse. The Manciple doubles his insults. He then reconsiders his position, since he and the Cook are apparently professionally associated and the Cook could retaliate by revealing things the Manciple does not want known. He therefore suggests that they placate the Cook with more wine. This tactic works, and the Manciple then tells his tale.

When the ancient Phoebus lived on the earth, he was a wondrous man, greatly to be admired. He kept a pet crow which he taught to speak. This crow was snow white and sang beautifully.

Phoebus also had a gorgeous wife whom he loved and tried to please, but he did not trust her. There was something in her personality which warned the young god that his wife might prove unfaithful.

(After giving this background information, the Manciple digresses to remind the listeners that anyone who is naturally evil, licentious, or untrustworthy will behave that way no matter what is done for him. He tries to prove with classical examples that a person's nature cannot be changed.)

The wife of Phoebus did have an unfaithful nature; she had a lover whom she entertained frequently. One day she took the man into her marriage bed while Phoebus was away. However, the white crow saw everything. When Phoebus returned the crow revealed the entire sordid episode. In his rage, Phoebus murdered his wife.

Phoebus at once regretted his rash action. In his grief, he turned on the crow, cursing him. Phoebus plucked out all the white feathers and condemned him to be black; he took away the bird's lovely song and his ability to speak and threw him to the devil. Ever since then, all crows have been black and can utter only a single ugly sound.

As a conclusion, the Manciple warns the company to keep silence; never to tell all they know lest it come back to ruin them. No man, he says, has ever been hurt by saying too little, but many have been ruined by talking too much.

Analysis

Unlike the Miller and the Reeve, or the Friar and the Summoner, the Manciple and the Cook do not take their feud beyond the prologue itself. This segment functions merely as an amusing interlude.

The story of Phoebus, his unfaithful wife, and the transformation of the crow comes from an ancient origin myth Chaucer must have encountered in the writings of Ovid. As in most myths, the central character is divine. The origin of the modern crow is explained by the god's actions upon the crow of the myth, changing him from white to black.

The theme of the story as it originated dealt with the terrible consequences of marital infidelity; but as in so many of the tales, Chaucer makes a profound change here. As the Manciple concludes, the theme of the tale becomes the foolishness to revealing all and the wisdom of keeping silent. It is appropriate to convey this theme from the mouth of the Manciple when one remembers that the Manciple stopped taunting the Cook for fear of what the Cook could reveal about him.

Study Questions

1. Another rivalry among the characters is revealed in the prologue to The Manciple's Tale. Between whom is this new rivalry and what is its basis?

2. Into what genre does The Manciple's Tale fall?

3. What is the theme of this tale?

4. Why is it appropriate for the Manciple to tell this particular tale?

5. How is the Cook calmed and persuaded not to argue further with the Manciple?

6. What did Phoebus' crow look like before he was cursed?

7. How was his appearance changed after he was cursed?

8. What specifically did the bird do which so angered Phoebus?

9. How does the behavior of Phoebus' wife relate her to other women in the *Tales*?

10. What is the Manciple's private commentary about human nature midway through the tale?

Answers

1. The newly introduced rivalry is between the Cook and the Manciple.

2. It is based in myth.

3. The foolishness of revealing all and the wisdom of keeping silent.

4. The Manciple's own wife has made him very unhappy.

5. He is given more wine.

6. He was a beautiful white bird who could talk and sing.

7. He is black. He can no longer talk or sing; he can only "caw."

8. He told Phoebus of the affair Phoebus' wife was having with another man.

9. There are several unfaithful wives in the various tales.

10. He says that it is nearly impossible to change human nature.

Suggested Essay Topics

1. What further commentary about marriage do the Manciple's private remarks and this tale give?

2. Explain the elements of myth in this tale.

The Parson's Tale

Summary

The journey of the pilgrims is almost over as this interlude begins. The Parson wants to remind the travelers that life itself is a spiritual journey, but the Parson says that he declines to bury his message in a fable. He will speak out exactly what he means. Promising to be brief, the Parson begins his tale.

The Parson openly preaches a sermon on the nature of penitence. First of all he discusses the concept of contrition. He describes the requirements for confession and details how satisfaction for sin is to be made. This incredibly long discourse becomes a sort of handbook for the sinner who wishes to obtain God's forgiveness according to the teachings of the Catholic Church.

Analysis

The Parson refuses to sink to the level of an entertainer as the Host seems to be demanding in the prologue. Remaining true to his devout and serious nature, the Parson takes a religious stance, yet promises to tell a merry story.

Not only does the Parson not tell a story, he preaches a two-hour sermon. The material in The Parson's Tale is very difficult for the modern reader to relate to; the pilgrims must have had an even more difficult time understanding. Yet the long sermon is in keeping with the character of the teller whose primary motivation, we are told, is the salvation of souls.

In constructing this treatise on penitence, Chaucer used the theological writings of prominent and revered theologians, heavily peppering their ideas with scriptural quotations. This source material sprang up after 1215 AD when confession became a requirement for forgiveness in the Catholic Church. The writings Chaucer used originated during this period so that the clergy would be thoroughly instructed and could educate the laity in this important area of practice.

Study Questions

1. How is the long sermon of the Parson appropriate to his character?

2. What is the theme of The Parson's Tale?

3. What are the sources Chaucer used in constructing this tale?

4. What kind of story were the Host and the pilgrims expecting from the Parson?

5. What comparison does the Parson make in his prologue?

6. Why does the Parson refuse to tell a fable?

7. In what genre is this tale written?

8. What requirement necessitated the clergy to instruct the laity about penitence?

9. What kind of handbook might The Parson's Tale comprise?

10. At what stage of the journey is The Parson's Tale presented?

Answers

1. He is a very sincere man who cares only about saving souls.

2. The nature of penitence is the theme of this tale.

3. Chaucer used clerical writings on this subject and scriptural quotations as sources.

4. They were expecting a merry tale.

5. Life is like a journey (or, in this case, a pilgrimage).

6. He says he will not hide his message in a lowly fable.

7. It is a sermon.

8. The Church began to require confession, the oral telling of sins to a priest.

9. A handbook for the sinner who wishes to obtain forgiveness.

10. They have almost completed the journey.

Suggested Essay Topics

1. Explain how the Parson might justify telling a sermon when he had promised a merry tale.

2. Discuss in detail the way The Parson's Tale fits the description of him in the General Prologue.

Chaucer's Retraction

Summary

Chaucer tells the reader that *The Canterbury Tales* are meant to give an overview of human nature; to be an encyclopedia of human behavior. The author does not want to be seen as a judge of his fellow man, but merely as a recorder of what he has heard and observed. He hopes that even the bawdy tales may be a means of improving his readers' souls.

Chaucer adds his thanks to God, to the Virgin Mary, and to the saints for their inspiration in the writing of his more spiritual works. He begs for the grace of true penitence and the blessing of a happy death.

Analysis

The nature of the retraction—a sincere statement to the reader—precludes analysis.

Sample Analytical Paper Topics

The following paper topics are designed to test your understanding of the work as a whole and to analyze important themes and literary devices. Following each question is a sample outline to help you get started.

Topic #1

One of Chaucer's persistent themes throughout *The Canterbury Tales* is the relationships of husbands and wives. In a well-developed paper, present the different views of this relationship as they are reflected in the *Tales*.

Outline

I. Thesis Statement: *One fine example of the diversity of* The Canterbury Tales *is its presentation of different views on the relationships of husbands and wives—both the traditional medieval (in which the woman is considered to be subject to her husband) and nontraditional (in which the wife controls her husband by any means possible).*

II. The Traditional View

    A. The Cleric's Tale

    B. The Franklin's Tale

    C. The Merchant's Tale

III. The Nontraditional View

    A. The Wife of Bath's Tale

    B. The Shipman's Tale

IV. The Problem of Unfaithful Wives

    A. The Miller's Tale

    B. The Merchant's Tale

V. Commentary on marriage in the dialogue between the tales

Topic #2

As the pilgrimage progresses, animosities develop between several pairs of characters. Discuss the feuds between the Miller and the Reeve; the Friar and the Summoner; and the Cook and the Host. In each explanation, include the origin of the rivalry or disagreement; the way tales are used as weapons in the dispute; what is added in the links of dialogue; and any hints from the General Prologue.

Outline

I. Thesis Statement: *During the course of the pilgrimage, animosities develop between several pairs of characters. Of particular note are the Miller and the Reeve; the Friar and the Summoner; and the Cook and the Host. These characters often use their tales as a "weapon" to express their feelings about each other and their dispute.*

II. The Miller and the Reeve

    A. Origin of the dispute

    B. Disputing through the dialogues

    C. Using the tales as weapons

III. The Friar and the Summoner

    A. Origin of the dispute

    B. Disputing through the dialogues

    C. Using the tales as weapons

IV. The Host and the Cook

    A. Origin of the dispute

    B. Disputing through the dialogues

    C. Using the tales as weapons

Topic #3

Describe three of the literary genres represented in *The Canterbury Tales*. For each genre, select and describe an example from the *Tales*, showing how the particular tale displays the characteristics of that genre.

Outline

I. Thesis Statement: *The romance, the fabliau, and the beast fable are just three of the literary genres employed by Chaucer in* The Canterbury Tales. *By examining one tale in each of these genres, the reader can gain an understanding of the characterstics of the three genres.*

II. The Romance, Represented by The Knight's Tale

    A. Noble characters

    B. Courtly language

    C. Pageantry

    D. Trial by combat

III. The Fabliau, Represented by The Miller's Tale

    A. Common people

    B. Infidelity

    C. Tricks and deception

IV. The Beast Fable, Represented by The Nun's Priest's Tale

    A. Animals personifying humans

    B. Moral lesson taught

Topic #4

The Canterbury Tales is thought to give an accurate view of the way women were regarded in medieval England. Using the General Prologue, the tales themselves, and the dialogue among the pilgrims, explain the various attitudes towards women in Chaucer's day.

Outline

I.   Thesis Statement: The Canterbury Tales *is thought to provide an accurate representation of the various attitudes toward women in medieval women. The tales about women and love may be grouped in a way that several generalized views of women in Chaucer's day become clear.*

II. The Virtuous Woman

    A.   General description

    B.   Constance

    C.   Griselda

    D.   The Prioress

III. The Inherent Sinfulness of Woman

    A.   The Miller's Tale

    B.   The Merchant's Tale

    C.   The Shipman's Tale

IV. The Domineering Woman

    A.   The Wife of Bath (her prologue and tale)

    B.   The Host's Wife

V.   Chaucer's Commentary following The Cleric's Tale

SECTION FOUR

Bibliography

Bloom, Harold, ed., *Geoffrey Chaucer, Modern Critical Views*. New York: Chelsea House Publishers, 1985.

Cohen, Barbara, *Geoffrey Chaucer: Canterbury Tales*. New York: Lothrop, Lee & Shephard Books, 1988.

Cooper, Helen, *Oxford Guides to Chaucer: The Canterbury Tales*. London: Oxford University Press, 1989.

Lumiansky, R. M., *Chaucer's Canterbury Tales*. New York: Washington Square Press, Pocket Books, 1948.

————, *Of Sundry Folk: The Dramatic Principle in the Canterbury Tales*. Austin: The University of Texas Press, 1955.

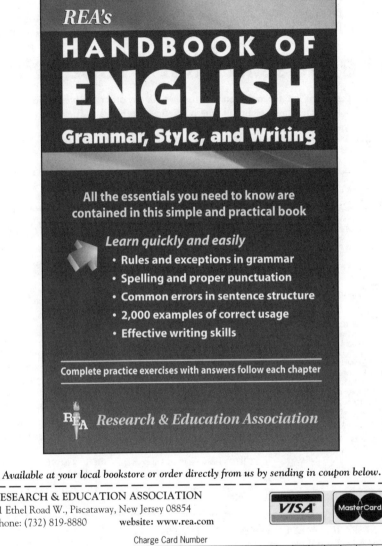

REA's Test Preps
The Best in Test Preparation

- REA "Test Preps" are **far more** comprehensive than any other test preparation series
- Each book contains up to **eight** full-length practice tests based on the most recent exams
- **Every** type of question likely to be given on the exams is included
- Answers are accompanied by **full** and **detailed** explanations

REA publishes over 60 Test Preparation volumes in several series. They include:

Advanced Placement Exams (APs)
Biology
Calculus AB & Calculus BC
Chemistry
Computer Science
English Language & Composition
English Literature & Composition
European History
Government & Politics
Physics
Psychology
Spanish Language
Statistics
United States History

College-Level Examination Program (CLEP)
Analyzing and Interpreting Literature
College Algebra
Freshman College Composition
General Examinations
General Examinations Review
History of the United States I
Human Growth and Development
Introductory Sociology
Principles of Marketing
Spanish

SAT II: Subject Tests
Biology E/M
Chemistry
English Language Proficiency Test
French
German
Literature

SAT II: Subject Tests (cont'd)
Mathematics Level IC, IIC
Physics
Spanish
United States History
Writing

Graduate Record Exams (GREs)
Biology
Chemistry
General
Literature in English
Mathematics
Physics
Psychology

ACT - ACT Assessment

ASVAB - Armed Services Vocational Aptitude Battery

CBEST - California Basic Educational Skills Test

CDL - Commercial Driver License Exam

CLAST - College-Level Academic Skills Test

ELM - Entry Level Mathematics

ExCET - Exam for the Certification of Educators in Texas

FE (EIT) - Fundamentals of Engineering Exam

FE Review - Fundamentals of Engineering Review

GED - High School Equivalency Diploma Exam (U.S. & Canadian editions)

GMAT - Graduate Management Admission Test

LSAT - Law School Admission Test

MAT - Miller Analogies Test

MCAT - Medical College Admission Test

MTEL - Massachusetts Tests for Educator Licensure

MSAT - Multiple Subjects Assessment for Teachers

NJ HSPA- New Jersey High School Proficiency Assessment

PPST - Pre-Professional Skills Tests

PSAT - Preliminary Scholastic Assessment Test

SAT I - Reasoning Test

SAT I - Quick Study & Review

TASP - Texas Academic Skills Program

TOEFL - Test of English as a Foreign Language

TOEIC - Test of English for International Communication

RESEARCH & EDUCATION ASSOCIATION
61 Ethel Road W. • Piscataway, New Jersey 08854
Phone: (732) 819-8880   **website: www.rea.com**

Please send me more information about your Test Prep books

Name _____

Address _____

City _____ State _____ Zip _____